Thank God For Trouble

Lessons Learned During My Cancer Journey

Marcia Lewis, LMFT, LCSW

ISBN: 9798374744606

Imprint: Independently published

Names have been changed to protect the privacy of individuals. The events written in the book are memories from the writer's perspective.

All scriptures are from the New Living Translation or King James Version.

Printed by: Amazon

First printing edition 2023

Publisher Address

www.realtalkandrealkwalk.com

Table of Contents

Dedication

For my husband who supports all my crazy ideas including this one.
For all my children who make "Fambly Time" so special.

Acknowledgments

Thank you to my dear husband, Ernie, whose love sparked the first lesson of what unconditional love looks like.

I want to give a special thanks to my son, Jared Lewis, who encouraged, gently critiqued, and motivated me on every step of this writing process.

Thank you to my daughter, Rachel, who was my graphic designer.

Thank you to my children, Camille, and Shiloh who were my support during the journey and my cheerleaders during the writing.

Thank you to my mother, Patricia Dennis, and father, Bezwick Dennis (deceased), who taught my sister, Karen, and I the importance of family.

Thank you to my aunt, Maureen Grange, who is my example of unwavering faith.

Thank you to the La Puente Church of Christ members who collectively are my "church family" and who I have learned so much from over the years.

Thank you to Shawntaye Smith and Marilyn Montgomery who sacrificed time to read and discuss my draft with me.

Thank you to my editor, Megan Joseph, who took my very flawed manuscript and created an actual book.

Finally thank you to everyone who has ever been a part of my life because you are part of every lesson God has ever revealed to me.

Introduction

Cancer.

The one word no one ever wants to hear. Any other diagnosis seemed more bearable than cancer because that disease carried the real possibility of death.

Every time I heard someone was diagnosed with cancer, I immediately felt a knot in my stomach, worry lines appeared on my forehead, and the words, "Oh no," rushed out.

Because of one very unusual symptom, I knew I had cancer before the doctor confirmed my diagnosis. There was just no other explanation. Of course, Dr. Google also supported my suspicions. In fact, I made an appointment for a second opinion at City of Hope in Duarte, CA before I received my official diagnosis.

When cancer was confirmed, I had the same reaction as when others were diagnosed; the knot in my stomach solidified, the worry lines, the tears, and the words, "Oh no," formed.

When I received the haunting phone call my husband, Ernie, was with me and my first statement to him after I hung up was simply, "I don't want to die." I had too many plans and milestones in life I wanted to experience and accomplish.

At the time of my diagnosis, only one of my four children was married, and I had yet to have any grandchildren. I was still working full time, and I had serious travel plans when I retired. Dying was just not in the realm of possibility for me, and I needed God to go along with my plans.

I decided very quickly I would not die. Not only would I not die, but I would survive, thrive, and conquer this major trial God allowed me to experience. I would not allow my mind to meditate on the very real possibility I might die. That line of thinking led to a very dark place I did not want to go to. From previous dives into the dark place, I knew once I allowed my mind to go there, it would be very difficult to climb back out. We have choices, even in the face of great trials, to dwell on the worst possible outcome or the best. I chose to focus on the best outcome.

Although painful in various ways, storms make a spiritual staircase, allowing us to step closer to God.

I also recognized my cancer diagnosis was a new journey God allowed me to be on with lessons He wanted me to learn. I made the decision to look for God and I found Him by focusing on what I might learn while on this road. My faith helped me shift my mindset and remove the worry of death. Even though I knew cognitively many people with faith died from cancer every day, I had no feeling or thought that was God's course for me. I believed the verse from John 11:4 applied.

But when Jesus heard about it he said, "Lazarus's sickness will not end in death. No, it happened for the glory of God so that the Son of God will receive glory from this." John 11:4 (NLT).

With my shield of faith firmly in hand, I began to try and ask the difficult question of "Why?"

Now, I didn't ask that question as a form of escape but as a form of self-education. As a teacher and servant of God, I knew He would open my eyes to things I never would have the opportunity to experience had I not been diagnosed with cancer. I knew I would have opportunities to testify during my journey and after God brought me through. I looked forward to receiving the lessons of wisdom God had in store for me. The decision to look for God and look for the lessons, I believe, was the most powerful decision I made on my journey. Without that decision, I would have been at the mercy of every negative thought, doubt, frustration, or fear that entered my mind. The Bible teaches:

Dear brothers and sisters, when troubles of any kind come your way, consider it an opportunity for great joy. For you know that when your faith is tested, your endurance has a chance to grow. So let it grow, for when your endurance is fully developed, you will be perfect and complete, needing nothing. James 1:2-4 (NLT).

I remember reading this passage in my youth and thinking, this makes no sense! *Why would I be happy about going through trials, pain, and misery? How could this ever be a good thing?*

Time is a perfect teacher. As I grew and experienced different trials, I came to understand there are great lessons and opportunities to praise God for allowing the experience. Although painful in various ways, storms make a spiritual staircase, allowing us to step closer to God. There are times when lessons can only be received after experiencing something difficult. So, when God chose me to go through this difficult time, I tried hard to praise Him because I knew He had lessons and opportunities to testify waiting just for me. I was no longer in my youth when I received my cancer diagnosis, so my mind was able to transition to, "Okay, Lord, it is my turn."

We have choices, even in the face of great trials, to dwell on the worst possible outcome or the best.

I was fifty-eight years old when I was diagnosed with uterine cancer, and my years up to that point were good. Of course, there were bumps in the road, but regarding my health, I was very blessed. I work as a medical social worker and have met patients from all walks of life, backgrounds, and ages. I met many patients younger than me who were riddled with major illnesses and diseases, and patients my own age who struggled with things God saw fit to never put in my path. Every time I met an ill patient my age, I thanked God for preserving my health. So, when this diagnosis came, I quickly accepted that it was my turn.

I never asked the question, "Why me?" because the answer returns rapidly. "Why not me?" God never promised anyone good health. He did make this promise to us:

....God has said, "I will never leave you nor forsake you." Hebrews 13:5 (NLT).

This verse teaches God has not promised anyone fame, fortune, or good health, but He has promised to never leave us alone. He will never turn His back on us.

But what does this mean?

How does God help when He is not physically by our side?

I believe every situation we endure is an opportunity to grow our faith, and faith is a choice. We have a choice to look at our circumstances and all the bleak looking physical data points, or we can focus our eyes on God and God alone. This book is my attempt to capture the lessons God revealed to me while I chose to focus on Him.

I believe every situation we endure is an opportunity to grow our faith, and faith is a choice.

For those who may not be believers, I hope my journey will clarify the purpose of faith. We believe we have a reward waiting in the end and that there are benefits to help us maneuver this thing called life. Often, Christianity may seem all tradition and rules without any real benefits. I hope my journey, struggles, and dependence on my faith show the benefits and blessings awaiting those who choose to believe in the power of God.

One

The Knowing

"However, no one knows the day or hour when these things will happen, not even the angels in heaven or the Son himself. Only the Father knows." Matthew 24:36 (NLT).

You never know beforehand how God is going to reveal truths to you. You never know how long your journey will be. You never know the size or intensity of all the things you will experience while on your journey. Those unknowns can be the scariest and most uncomfortable places to exist. But if you are a follower of Christ, you know God hears your prayers and will answer accordingly. As a follower of Christ, you also know trials are a part of our Christian journey.

The first change I noticed after I began this journey was in my prayer life. I have always fought against praying for physical things, it just troubled me constantly. My aversion to these types of prayers got to the point where I would get frustrated with prayers I heard in the assembly because they seemed to focus mostly on the physical requests of members. That frustration would carry over and sit with me, and I would hold secret frustrations with members who constantly had prayer requests for their tests, surgeries, pains, etcetera.

I even backed up my frustration with biblical examples, like the prayers of Paul. Paul suffered many hardships, but it was rare he asked for physical blessings. Instead, he focused on the needs of others, demonstrating what I believed was an understanding God would grant him whatever he needed. I taught my high school classes, and later on women's classes, that we should try to focus our prayers on the spiritual characteristics of God and the fruit of the spirit because these were things God promised we could have without limit.

But the Holy Spirit produces this kind of fruit in our lives: love, joy, peace, patience, kindness, goodness, faithfulness, gentleness, and self-control. There is no law against these things! Galatians 5:22-23 (NLT).

After all those years I silently criticized the prayer requests of others, I found myself in the same position. I felt a twinge of guilt when I began praying about my cancer. I felt like a hypocrite for focusing so much on my physical condition and asking others to focus their prayers on it as well. Now my prayers for physical things were right alongside everyone else's. I had never focused so much prayer on my physical wellbeing and truthfully, it felt very awkward. Even with all of those feelings of hypocrisy and awkwardness, I found I couldn't help but pray for my physical health. When I look back, it only made sense; whatever dominated your mind was what you prayed for.

Suddenly, I understood why all those members requested prayer after prayer for their physical ailments. *Who else would you turn to with those concerns? What else were you going to do?* When faced with uncertainty, you long for something unmovable, something to bring a sense of peace and comfort to your spirit. You want to know God is with you. Afterall, God instructed us:

Give all your worries and cares to God, for He cares about you. 1 Peter 5:7 (NLT).

Somehow, I developed a false belief that God had enough on His plate, and I should not add my little human concerns to the more important things He had going on.

How wrong I was.

Because of my limited human brain, I placed limitations on God. The truth is, God does not have a plate for concerns that can ever get too crowded nor a limit to the concerns He can handle.

In the movie *Bruce Almighty*, Bruce complains to God about how poorly He is doing His job. To see how Bruce would handle the powers of God, He gave Bruce powers to try to do God's job. Eventually, Bruce got so tired of all the prayer requests he said, "Yes," to everything to make it easier on himself, but that caused even more problems. All of the troubles that happened were because Bruce was human. We humans are flawed and as far from perfect as possible. Thankfully, God does not act like or respond like Bruce or any other human. God does not get tired or have a limit to what He will handle in a day.

We can see how beautifully unlike humans God actually is when we look at the profound answer He gave to Paul when he prayed for physical healing.

... to keep me from becoming proud, I was given a thorn in my flesh, a messenger from Satan to torment me and keep me from becoming proud. Three different times I begged the Lord to take it away. Each time He said, "My grace is all you need. My power works best in weakness." So now I am glad to boast about my weaknesses, so that the power of

Christ can work through me. That's why I take pleasure in my weaknesses, and in the insults, hardships, persecutions, and troubles I suffer for Christ. For when I am weak, then I am strong. 2 Corinthians 12:7-10 (NLT).

Right there in verse nine the Bible says, "My power works best in weakness." So, we will not experience the greatest power from God until we are at our weakest!

This was mind blowing to me. It is only when I am at my weakest I can truly experience the powerful strength of the Almighty to provide what I need spiritually to get through what I am going through physically.

This is the exact opposite of what we are taught. Our natural selves say to never give up control because when you do, others will take advantage of you. It is very difficult to switch to a mindset that says, "I want to give up control of my life so God can take control."

Thank you, Lord, for the lesson.

The truth is, God does not have a plate for concerns that can ever get too crowded nor a limit to the concerns He can handle.

So, there I was with this gigantic physical trial, unsure of what was going to happen, how I got there, or how to proceed. This was the biggest physical trial of my life and in the lives of my family, so the only option I believed to be helpful was to go to God in prayer about it! This first lesson on prayer was how I knew God was with me and it reinforced that God would never forsake me - because I relearned I could go to Him in prayer about every big and small issue in my life. That was how I had peace while going through the challenge. I wanted what was best for me physically and spiritually. I wanted health and I wanted to please God.

We pray because we want God's will to align with ours. In other words, we want God to agree with everything we ask for, without considering His plans for us. How many prayers does God hear asking Him to bend His will? The number is unanswerable, but this question shouts: How often are we willing to bend our will to please God? How often are we willing to say, "Not my will but thine?"

I have thought, *how many other children of the Lord have asked for healing and instead God chose to take them home?* When our faith matures, we understand that if God chooses death for us and we believe everything God does is good, then He has decided death is best for us.

It is only when I am at my weakest I can truly experience the powerful strength of the Almighty to provide what I need spiritually to get through what I am going through physically.

This is an extremely big, hard, difficult, ugly pill to swallow. My human mind cannot comprehend how death would be best for me. *How is that possible?* If I die, I cannot give God anymore praise with my life. I cannot help to spread the gospel of Christ any further. I cannot visit the sick, I cannot teach, I cannot do anything. However, we need to humble ourselves. Every incident that occurs in life is not just a lesson for you, but for others who may know you. Every life is a classroom with lessons for others to receive, either good or bad.

If you are a parent, consider how your children learned from you without you saying anything. Children learn much more from observation than from direct teaching. And so it is in life - others will learn lessons just by observing your life and potentially your death. Death is necessary for others to measure their own life and understand the importance of having a right relationship with God, because everyone must die someday.

Death is the worst outcome imaginable for most because we do not fully understand what happens *after* death. But to God, death is just a part of His complete plan. This insight goes both ways. Many people suffer unimaginable tragedies and believe death would be a welcome end to the pain, suffering, and abuse. But even in this, God has a plan for you to develop a relationship with Him so He can give you hope for this life, and in the life to come.

Emotionally, I cannot tolerate thinking about the millions of innocent children and adults who suffer terrible abuse at the hands of another. These thoughts can send me into a deep depression because I cannot make sense of it. Other deaths are more palatable.

When criminals die, we may think they got what they deserved, this is palatable. But when a respectable person dies, it forces us to acknowledge good people die, too. We all need to consider where we want our eternal destination to be. I think of those martyrs who declare their faith in God while in non-Christian countries, knowing death is a real threat based on their declaration of faith. Consider what mental turmoil one must go through to declare faith in God knowing you will probably be jailed, tortured, or even killed.

I think of kamikaze suicide bombers who willingly choose to die for their country. What mental exercises must one practice to be willing to sacrifice their life for a cause? These thoughts make me realize I have been so sheltered from these types of threats in this country and therefore, I have never had to look the possibility of death in the face and accept it.

The possibility of death was always distant, a cruise ship on the horizon, or a soft melody heard from the street. Then, suddenly, I was diagnosed with what the World Health Organization calls a leading cause of death worldwide: CANCER. After I cried for a bit, I realized even if my prognosis came back poor, my God was still in charge. Regardless of what the diagnosis and prognosis were, I knew if it was His will for me to recover then He would cure me, no matter what.

"Please Lord, let me be in the group You choose to heal. I know You love me, but can You give me more time on this side of life?" Was it selfish of me to ask God to let me stay here and delay my trip to Him? Was He offended I didn't want to rush home to be with Him? I do not have the spiritual maturity of Paul yet, who said:

For to me to live is Christ, and to die is gain. Philippians 1:21 (NLT).

I also have not gone through all the physical trials Paul went through in order to develop this attitude. At that point, my mind was in a quandary. "For to live is Christ," means I must experience more trials, and my death ends all future trials!

Every life is a classroom with lessons for others to receive, either good or bad.

My human brain responds, "I'll take my chances." My human brain says, "Let me continue to suffer here and face trials on earth because earth is all I know."

I have read about heaven and the pearly gates, but honestly, I'm in no rush to get there. I want what we all want, to live to a ripe old age of one hundred, then go to sleep and never wake up. But alas, life rarely turns out the way we plan. As a Christian, I take comfort, hope, and joy in the belief that God's plans are always better than mine, even if I cannot see them. I could not see cancer, but I intentionally believed God, who saw all and had my best interest in mind.

Soon after we received the cancer diagnosis, my husband and I were scheduled for a weekend getaway. Ernie had always been good at planning our trips. These vacations were one of the many experiences I enjoyed and wanted to continue. This weekend trip was with our dear travel friends, and it was scheduled before we received the diagnosis, so it was good timing. I remember having a completely new and different outlook as I walked the pier in Oceanside, CA with Ernie. I wanted to shout, "Hey people, I have cancer!"

I had this hurdle ahead of me and it felt odd that no one knew of my burden unless I told them. Everyone passed by us as if nothing major was going on in my life. I realized all over again you never really know what someone was going through. No one wore a sign for you to know their struggle. As I walked that pier, I realized they did not know what I was going through, and I didn't know what they were going through. My perspective quickly changed to one of empathy for others around me because they might have a grave diagnosis, too. She might be going through a divorce, or he might be raising difficult teenagers. They might be unemployed and financially struggling.

It made me want to pray for others who were also suffering with their own trials. Dealing with my own physical trial made me more sympathetic to the physical trials of others. I was more willing to pray for physical healing because of what I was going through. Already, I recognized cancer made me more aware and sympathetic to the struggles of others because I was now faced with my own struggles. *Thank you, God, for opening my eyes to my need to be more sympathetic and patient with others. Thank you, Lord, for the lesson.*

Take some time to meditate on what you experienced and how those experiences changed you. Look for the pearls of wisdom God is waiting to give you. On the other hand, if your trials have made you bitter, angry, depressed, anxious, hateful, fearful, or any other negative characteristic, I recommend you evaluate your relationship with the Lord. The Lord cannot add spiritual virtues to you if your spirit is not actively seeking Him. Without God, our natural self will respond naturally to trials, which leads to more fear and bitterness.

How do you want your character to develop? Most people do not want to be identified by their negative characteristics. Negative characteristics do not attract positive people, positive vibes, good energy, or spiritual growth. We must decide first what we want our character to be, then put a plan together to develop those good characteristics. There are many good and positive people in the world. However, only those positive people who are in right relationship with the Lord have the promise of eternal life.

Your Lessons Learned

1. What have your trials opened your eyes to?

____

____

____

____

2. What spiritual characteristics were sharpened because of what God allowed you to go through?

____

____

____

____

3. What natural characteristics must you change in order to glorify God for your trials and thank Him for loving you enough to teach you how to be more like Him?

____

____

____

____

Two

The Stillness

"Be still and know I am God! I will be honored by every nation. I will be honored throughout the world." The Lord of Heaven's Armies is here among us; the God of Israel is our fortress. Psalm 46:10 (NLT).

The world should have stopped when I received my diagnosis, but it did not. Everything around me continued on as normal, but I was no longer normal. There was no announcement on the television that Marcia had cancer, no plane writing out my diagnosis in the sky. There was no viral video that took the world by storm. Instead, everyone went on with their lives as if a jaw dropping, world crumbling, horrifying and terrifying event had not just occurred.

Truthfully, me being consumed with worry was no reason the rest of the world needed to be. There was no reason the rest of the world needed to change their plans or work on the timeline I thought was necessary and reasonable. Early on, it wore on my patience more than I expected. For my entire adult life, I *knew* I was a patient individual. In actuality, I *thought* I had patience until I was diagnosed with cancer, and the worry set in.

Worry and patience are like fire and ice, water and oil, or God and Satan, they do not work well together. Early during this journey, I was spoiled with haste that matched my own. During the very first visit with my primary care doctor, the look of focus and gravity on Dr. Bryce's face and the speed with which she made follow-up appointments with specialists was astounding. Within one week I had three appointments, capped off with an in-office biopsy procedure.

Because Dr. Bryce moved with such speed, I assumed everything and everyone else would move at the same pace - but it was not to be. Instead, after that first week of efficiency, I felt like I was at the DMV waiting for my number to be called. My number was 235 and they had just called sixty-two. You know the feeling of waiting for your number to be called, when you perk up every time the speaker starts, but fall back into your chair when you realize it's not your number? That was how I felt every time my phone rang.

God revealed to me patience cannot have a timeline or an endpoint.

After my first two appointments, I had my biopsy on a Friday and the doctor stated she would call me the following Tuesday with the results. A four-day turnaround for biopsy results sounded reasonable to me. On Tuesday, I woke up excited and anxious to get my results. I felt myself getting more nervous as I watched the clock's hands pass ten o'clock but reasoned it was still relatively early. My fingers tapped on my desk in time with the ticking clock as the morning stretched into lunchtime. I waited well into the afternoon before I called the doctor to get results. The receptionist said, "Results are usually not back that quickly, so maybe call by Friday."

I suddenly felt surprised, frustrated, and angry before asking, "Then why did the doctor tell me Tuesday?" The receptionist did not have a good answer.

I went through Wednesday and Thursday somewhat calmly since I was told to wait until Friday, though, I did have thoughts like, *this is so cruel! Don't you people know I am waiting to hear if I will live or die? Hey, medical staff, I MIGHT HAVE CANCER! DON'T YOU CARE?*

I waited until four-thirty p.m. on Friday before calling the doctor, and then heard, "Your results are here but the doctor went home already, and only the doctor can give you the results."

Are you serious? What kind of unfeeling, unsympathetic doctor left someone all weekend to worry about their fate from cancer? My mind raced through different scenarios to make sense of what I was experiencing.

The doctor left early to watch her kid's soccer game.

Maybe someone in her family was sick.

Maybe her house was burning down.

Maybe someone tried to steal her mother's credit card information and was booking trips to Florida.

Whatever the reason, clearly, she must have had some type of emergency. My mind would not let me accept the thought, *she does not care.* However hard my mind tried to make sense of my predicament, there was no use arguing with the receptionist and all I could say was, "Thank you."

The doctor called the following Monday morning at nine-thirty a.m. with the news. She made a conscious decision not to give me my results on Friday because she did not want to spoil my weekend. That was the wrong rationale for me since all I was able to do was think about the results of the biopsy. However, I understood she believed she was doing me a favor.

I am the type of person who says, "Give me the bad news first so I can begin to deal with it. Rip the bandage off quickly so I can see the injury." How does someone maintain a sense of peace in their heart when it feels like their life is hanging in the balance? How was I supposed to enjoy my weekend while I waited for the verdict? I would much rather have heard the news and had time to process it. Even though it was not my preference, I saw God was working on me at that moment. I wanted the information when I wanted it, yet all I could do was return to God in prayer every time my thoughts strayed to worrying about "The Call."

God revealed to me patience cannot have a timeline or an endpoint. I was patient until Tuesday when I was supposed to get my results, then until Friday when I was supposed to get my results. When the results did not come, my patience was gone.

Do you remember the cartoon *the Roadrunner?* Do you remember how quickly he said, "Beep, beep" then ran away frustrating the coyote even more? That is how quickly my patience ran away when I failed to get the answers I wanted when I wanted them. I realized I was waiting on the wrong doctor. I realized I had an opportunity to develop the ability to wait on God, not on man. It was very difficult for me not to be anxious when things were not falling into place the way I expected them to. In that difficult time, I learned feelings of anxiety are a reminder my faith is not in God at the moment, but the anxiety was a result of faith in man or myself. *Thank you God for the lesson.*

As our relationship with God grows, the peace guarding our hearts also grows.

A simple definition of anxiety is worrying about future events. Depression is worrying about past events. We become anxious when we worry about what may happen next. We feel depression when we are sad about what has already happened. In both instances, we have an opportunity to turn to the Lord and ask for peace because we have no power to change the past or the future.

This is another level of faith I have not yet attained. It is the ability to worry, pray, then leave the issue with God so I can enjoy my weekend. I love the scripture:

Always be full of joy in the Lord. I say it again—rejoice! Let everyone see you are considerate in all you do. Remember, the Lord is coming soon. Don't worry about anything; instead, pray about everything. Tell God what you need and thank him for all he has done. Then you will experience God's peace, which exceeds anything we can understand. His peace will guard your hearts and minds as you live in Christ Jesus. Philippians 4:4-7 (NLT).

This passage reminds me rejoicing is a choice. It is a conscious decision to be glad no matter what your circumstances are. I am still praying I learn how to do this. I am not able to say and believe, "I have cancer and I choose joy." As time went on, I believe I eventually arrived at the point where I was able to choose to focus more on my faith, my God, my family, and less on my cancer. I could be at peace because of my belief God allowed this to occur, and God had a plan. I learned to lean into and fully trust in God's plan. There were times when I was unsure, or when I didn't understand, but I have learned even in those moments to lean on my faith and trust in God.

Relief from worry is waiting for you when you let your anxiety go and accept that God's got this.

The passage also speaks about God's peace that exceeds anything we can understand. God's peace will guard our hearts and minds as we live in Christ Jesus. This is the peace we all strive for. This is the peace that does not change due to our life's circumstances. This is the peace only found in God. As our relationship with God grows, the peace guarding our hearts also grows. I believe attaining this peace is part of spiritual maturity. I envision that with it, the world can crumble around me, but I will feel only peace because I know God is handling everything out of my control. As Paul said,

I don't mean to say I have already achieved these things or I have already reached perfection. But I press on to possess that perfection for which Christ Jesus first possessed me. No, dear brothers and sisters, I have not achieved it, but I focus on this one thing: Forgetting the past and looking forward to what lies ahead, I press on to reach the end of the race and receive the heavenly prize for which God, through Christ Jesus, is calling us. Philippians 3:12-14 (NLT).

I have not achieved the level of peace that allows me to have cancer and peace at the same time, but I know that is the goal. So, I press on toward achieving the ability to worry briefly about physical and worldly challenges then quickly resting in God's peace. I press on toward achieving the ability to have joy in my heart even when life takes a left turn out of my comfortable journey. This lesson of leaning on God is not one anyone can master after experiencing one event. It is formed over the course of multiple situations God places you in. Yet this was my experience in this moment toward my journey for God given peace.

The next dreaded thing I needed to do was tell my children. I decided early when I was going to doctor's appointments I did not want to tell anyone until I knew for sure. So, I did not tell the children because I did not want to worry anyone for nothing. This was a difficult decision to stick to because one daughter lived with me, and two other children visited often. Once we were all together and I almost let it slip. But the overwhelming thought was, *I do not want to see those worried faces until absolutely necessary*. When the diagnosis was confirmed, we reached out to the kids, told them we had important news and scheduled a zoom meeting as soon as possible.

By ten-thirty a.m., the same day I received the diagnosis, I was sitting in front of the computer looking at the beautiful faces of my four children and daughter-in-law and hated to give them this news. I did not want to watch their faces turn from happy to sad in an instant. I did not want to see the look of shock, the worry lines, and the visible thought, *oh no, Mom has cancer*. But here we were.

I talked, my husband talked, and they cried, which made me cry. My oldest son and his wife said they were flying home for the surgery. I asked, "Why?" The gravity of my situation really had not hit me yet.

My son replied, "I'm not asking you, Mom." End of discussion.

After the biopsy, surgery, and back and forth with doctors, I started having trouble with the insurance authorizing my chemotherapy. This delayed my treatment by three weeks, and I was irate. Unfortunately, or maybe fortunately, I am not a confrontational person.

Others would tell me, "Marcia, you need to speak up and fight for yourself," but I would rather say I am waiting on God and feel all the anxiety internally instead of experiencing it externally in a confrontation. It is more anxiety provoking for me to try to bend someone else's will, than to stew in my own feelings. I found relief from my anxiety when I came to the realization that treatment would start when God says treatment would start and not before. It feels amazing to trust in the Lord, but the challenge is to keep my trust in God and not let my focus and faith bounce around from God, to doctors, to myself, and back again.

Trusting in the Lord is like holding your breath under water with the anticipation of a full breath when you break through the surface. Think of the relief you feel when you are able to breathe. Trusting in God is like breathing that sigh of relief. Relief from worry is waiting for you when you let your anxiety go and accept God's got this. Trusting in God is like a child running through a field of flowers without a care in the world because they know their parents are taking care of everything else. I was still working on leaning on God when He put me in another situation where I was not displaying patience or the ability to really be still and listen to Him.

After my first chemotherapy treatment, the side effects lasted about seven days. My first symptom the next morning was a strange brain fog that made my husband's words sound like the adults in a Charlie Brown cartoon. All of a sudden, his words sounded like, "Womp, whomp, whomp, whomp, whomp." I asked him to help me to the bed, and that is where I stayed for the next five days. I had no appetite and I was nauseous. Thankfully, I did not vomit this time, but I was extremely fatigued. By the seventh day, I began to feel somewhat normal.

So, I went to my next treatment with the expectation I would have symptoms for approximately seven days and then I would feel normal again. When the seven days turned into ten, and then twelve days, I was upset. I thought, *why is this treatment not responding like the last one? How can I plan anything, or even function if I don't know what tomorrow will bring?* God was showing me I was still trying to control this thing. I had to accept every treatment may look different, and I may not know what to expect or what the outcome would be. I had to remove my expectations, be still and depend on God.

How does one not put expectations on a situation? Knowing what will happen next gives us a sense of control. Yet, as a child of God I made the commitment to give up control of my life, and to allow God to take control. This situation highlighted that I had never truly submitted, but I have always figured out a way to maintain some level of control. In the midst of chemotherapy, I had no control of how long my side effects would be, what side effects I would have, or how I would respond to those side effects. God was teaching me how to be still and know He is God.

It felt like God had to totally strip me of my physical ability before I conceded I had no control, and He had all control. I felt very vulnerable when I bowed before God in a state of total abandon and cried, "Lord here I am, do as you will."

I went to sleep feeling sick and hoped when I awoke in the morning I would feel better. When that did not happen, I had to wait another day for God to do His will. Not knowing what was coming next was extremely unnerving. I could not prepare when I did not know what was coming. This was a state of total surrender because the medicine was in my body doing whatever it was supposed to do, and I could not control it. My body was experiencing symptoms I had only received a brief overview of. The oncologist gave some printed material on each drug I would receive during chemotherapy and told me to read them. But no amount of paper could really prepare me for what was coming, and I could not control that. I felt like I was at the mercy of the disease, and I had no recourse but to wait and pray.

A port-a-cath was placed into the right atrium of my heart to administer the chemotherapy drugs. I was worried about my heart and the strong medication they were going to pump through it. I was told the medication was too strong to go into other veins and often caused them to collapse. Immediately I asked, "Then why direct it through my heart?"

The nurse assured me the biggest collection of blood is in the heart and my blood would carry the medication throughout the body more quickly. This did not give me much comfort. My blood reacted negatively from the very first treatment, and eventually, I started having heart problems. But this harsh treatment saved my life. As the medications traveled through my veins, they killed all the cancer cells, but they also killed healthy cells. The hope was the body was strong enough to withstand this beating, and after treatments were complete, the good cells would regenerate, and the cancer cells would be gone. I had to acknowledge the blessing of my healthy body even though I was being treated for a disease that could kill it. I learned there were some cancer patients so reactive to chemotherapy they had to be admitted to the hospital to be cared for by nurses for every treatment.

It felt like God had to totally strip me of my physical ability before I conceded I had no control and He had all control.

In the past when nurses took my vitals, I never paid attention. My rationale was they would let me know when something was of concern and then I would pay attention. When a person goes through chemotherapy you must give blood approximately eight days after each treatment and two days before the next treatment so the oncologist can evaluate your blood levels. The correct levels allow you to take your next treatment. With each passing week and each additional vial of blood taken, I continued to nonchalantly pay attention to these tests. All of that changed when the nurse called and informed me I was neutropenic. I replied, "Neutro what?"

She went on to explain my white blood count was extremely low, and I basically had no immune system. She informed me not to leave the house, not to allow anyone in the house, to stay away from my dogs, and have all the utensils used to prepare my food sterilized! The treatment was to go to the clinic for the next three days to receive a shot to raise my immune system. *So much for not leaving the house.*

After my next treatment I was informed in addition to being neutropenic, my red blood cells were low, my hemoglobin was low, and I needed a blood transfusion. This led to two visits to the emergency room and one failed blood transfusion due to an allergic reaction. Although I did not get the full unit of blood due to the reaction, it was enough to raise my levels just enough so I could have my next treatment.

An interesting dynamic occurs during treatment. Even though no one wants cancer, and no one wants to go through chemotherapy, once you are told you must have chemotherapy you want to finish your treatments as quickly and smoothly as possible. A delay in receiving a treatment is a delay in finishing.

It was nerve-racking to realize the thing meant to make me healthy was making me sicker. I was frustrated I had to have so many visits to the emergency room, but I told myself at least we were back on track with chemotherapy.

After my next chemotherapy treatment, my levels fell again, and I had to receive two more units of blood. This time they gave me medication to reduce the risk of another allergic reaction. Essentially, blood is extremely vital and without it you die. Not exactly something I should have been ignoring and I started to see the benefit of paying attention to what my blood was doing. I never had to think so much about my blood or understand the complexities of it.

After my last of six chemotherapy treatments, there were lingering physical symptoms stopping me from returning to my previous level of physical ability. My blood was polluted and my heart was experiencing symptoms I had never felt before. I felt a sort of pain or pressure in

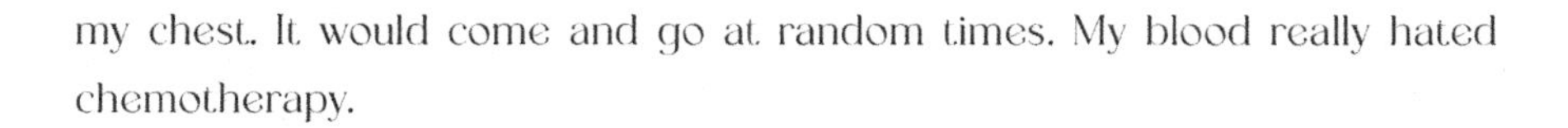

my chest. It would come and go at random times. My blood really hated chemotherapy.

I was learning how to feel the symptom and then feel contentment in the Lord at the same time.

First, my white blood cells were affected, then the hemoglobin, and finally my platelet count. A normal platelet count is between 150,000 to 450,000 platelets per microliter of blood. After my last treatment, my platelet count was 48,000 but the nurse said just wait and repeat your labs in one week. After one week my platelet count decreased to 34,000. Again, the nurse called and said, "There is nothing we can do until your platelets are below 20,000. If your platelets drop below 20,000 you will need a blood transfusion. So, wait some more and repeat your labs in another week." I was instructed not to do anything that might cause me to bleed, like using knives or falling. Dr. Google added do not floss your teeth or play with your dogs. Basically, do not do anything that may introduce infection in your body. Thankfully, by my next labs, my platelets increased to 77,000 and continued to go in the right direction.

Interestingly, I do not recall having any major symptoms that alerted me to the fact that my blood was low in all counts. So, it was difficult to do nothing when I felt like I could do everything. Remember, I was the one who liked to stay busy and now the nurse said do nothing. Have you ever been with children who very quickly say, "I'm bored?" Well, I was one of those children who did not like to sit still, and television bored me if I was not doing something in addition to watching it. I felt totally bored and the only excitement I had was to watch paint dry.

Although the platelets were increasing, I had to face the daunting possibility I may never return to my previous level of health. Doctors had no immediate answers regarding my lingering symptoms, and I had to wait for more specialists. The technician who did the echocardiogram gave me some hope when he said, "If I saw something of concern, I would not be allowed to let you leave." Since I was allowed to leave, I understood whatever I was feeling in my heart was not currently life threatening.

Nonetheless, the blood and the heart are both extremely important and I found it difficult not to worry about the outcome of these symptoms and tests. God allowed me plenty of opportunity to practice waiting on Him because the follow-up appointment to the cardiologist was scheduled six weeks after my echocardiogram. Honestly, as time went on, I worried less about my heart, even though I still felt the symptoms of pain in my chest and shortness of breath if I overexerted myself. I thought *I may have heart issues, and blood issues but I am still alive.* I was learning how to feel the symptom and then feel contentment in the Lord at the same time.

There are so many things that can go wrong with the human body and God is aware of every single one of them. We typically become aware of problems within our bodies when things stop working correctly, but God is always aware of our physical and spiritual wellbeing. I believe in doctors and medicine because God allowed man to have the knowledge to be doctors and make medicine. But ultimately God is in control. When I am not stressing about the outcome of a situation, I can calmly say that. The challenge is being able *to be still* and *know God is in control*, even when you don't know the outcome of your problems, and you feel totally out of control. No matter what life may bring - war, pandemic, political unrest, illness, or poverty the highest level of spiritual maturity is to look at these real-life dilemmas and sleep peacefully at night knowing God is in control. The peace comes when you can truly wait on God without anxiety or worry about if or when He will hear and answer your prayers.

There are moments in life when we feel all alone because of what we are going through. I love my family very much, and I know they love me, but I was the only one receiving the chemotherapy treatments, and I was the only one suffering with the side effects. One can feel lonely in these instances. However, as a Christian I was never truly alone because I knew God was in control, and I just needed to wait on Him.

No matter what life may bring - war, pandemic, political unrest, illness, or poverty the highest level of spiritual maturity is to look at these real-life dilemmas and be able to sleep peacefully at night knowing God is in control.

Your Life Lessons

1. Consider those times you have felt anxious and ask yourself where was your faith at that moment?

____

____

____

____

2. Why is it difficult for you to be still and wait on God?

____

____

____

____

3. What is hindering you from letting go of the past, and grasping the peace God wants to give you?

____

____

____

____

Three

The Blessing

And my God will supply every need of yours according to His riches in glory in Christ Jesus. Philippians 4:19 (NLT).

At the time of my diagnosis, I had been married for thirty-seven years. During those thirty-seven years I was loving and faithful, as well as adventurous and independent. I loved trying new things and learning new skills. My husband was always, and still is, supportive of my hobbies and encourages me to pursue whatever idea blossoms in my mind. I decided I liked hiking, and he helped me buy my first set of hiking boots and poles. I even found time to hike on our vacations. He would take me to the hiking location and make his presence known to the strangers I would be walking with, as if to say, "This is my wife, and you better bring her back to me."

Somehow, I began fixing things around the house, which progressed into making small wood projects. This turned into my own "She Shed" for all my electrical tools and more space as my projects got bigger and bigger. My husband even had my shed decked out by raising the ceiling to make it more comfortable for me. I can tell my husband lives by the saying, "Happy wife, happy life," and I appreciate him for this. If making me happy makes him happy, who am I to argue? I won't fight him trying to make me happy! This is a Count Your Blessings moment. Sometimes you have to stop and acknowledge the good moments during tough times to give God praise for that blessing.

I also take great pleasure in taking care of everyone around me. I was the primary caregiver for all four children when they were growing up, and a caregiver to my husband through his various surgeries and medical conditions. Most recently, he had a hip surgery, and I was happy to take care of him. I remember he would say things to show his appreciation, and although I never responded negatively, I was always a little perturbed when he praised my efforts to care for him.

I felt his praise was not necessary because not only was I happy to take care of him, but it was also my wifely duty to do so. I would say, "I know you would do the same for me," and I believed that based on the unconditional love and support he showed me. But his continual compliments still bothered me, and I thought, *why are you complimenting me for something that is in my job description?* I also thought, *I don't need your praise to continue doing what I am doing.* On the other hand, I knew I would be upset if he never said anything. And then I got cancer.

Sometimes you have to stop and acknowledge the good moments during the tough times to give God praise for that blessing.

My husband wanted to be with me through every test, every treatment, every doctor's visit, scan, surgery, and everything else. And he was. He made it very clear whatever I needed or wanted he would make it his mission to provide, and he did. He was by my side holding me up in the early morning when I was vomiting. He rubbed my feet, my legs, and my hands when the bone pain and neuropathy became unbearable. He shaved my head when my hair began falling out and held me when I cried at the trauma of seeing my bald head for the first time. He decided on his own I needed a few respite weekends between chemotherapy treatments just to get away and change the scenery. I did not want all the fuss, but I appreciated those weekends very much. I began to see and experience my husband in a way I had never had the opportunity to experience before.

I experienced a dimension of love hidden from me because I never needed this before. Suddenly, he became my knight in shining armor and I appreciated every little thing he did for me. I appreciated his words of encouragement, and his caring spirit. I appreciated his thoughtfulness and his desire to provide everything I may want even before I knew I wanted or needed it. In my eyes he became the most beautiful man that ever existed, and I was overly thankful he was mine. Our love became fierce because we were united in our fight to beat cancer. The traditional wedding vows are *in sickness and in health*. For thirty-seven years I said, "Yes honey I will take care of you when you are sick," never imagining he would one day take care of me.

Whatever is in your heart prior to your trial will dictate how you respond to that trial. If you are already standing on the word of God, then the word of God will continue to direct your steps. However, if you are standing on your own merits, and trusting in your own physical, spiritual, and mental strength, then when those merits begin to deteriorate, your foundation will begin to crumble.

After I began my treatments, I started telling my husband how much I appreciated him. These words of appreciation and praise just began flowing out of me. They came from a place of need. I needed to say these words because the feeling of gratitude was so intense, I could not hold them in any longer. It was like scales fell from my eyes and I saw things I had never seen before, good things - blessings I never knew I had - a husband who loved me unconditionally.

Whatever is in your heart prior to your trial will dictate how you respond to that trial.

Every time I heard of a cancer patient who was not being treated well by their mate, I looked at my partner with even more love and appreciation. I joined an online cancer support group where the women would share what was going on in their lives. One woman shared with us her husband called her an "ugly cancer patient," and she wanted advice about what she could do to make herself more presentable to him. I was appalled and disgusted by the selfish man.

Another woman said she was worried about sharing her cancer diagnosis with her family because of how they would respond. She was right to be worried because when she told them they responded, "That is your problem not ours."

Another woman asked her daughter to take her to a doctor's appointment, and her daughter complained the entire time about how much this was an inconvenience for her. The worst one was a husband who divorced his wife after seventeen years of marriage to date the nurse who was treating his wife's cancer. I did not know such unfeeling, heartless people existed. I felt sorry for all these women who had to deal with the physical battle of cancer in addition to the emotional battle of insensitive and uncaring family members. Again, I looked at my husband and my family and said, "Thank you, God."

One day, I was thinking about how I previously did not care to hear my husband's praise about how I cared for him, but now I was praising him almost daily for taking care of me. I asked him how my words of praise made him feel, and he replied, "I just figured you needed to say them."

The light bulb went off in my head because I had never considered his words of praise to me were because he needed to say them. I then thought of our praise to God. I have learned over the years God has commanded us to praise Him for OUR benefit, not because God needs our praise. When we focus our mind on God we are reminded of His power and presence in our lives. Praising God is like biofeedback for your soul, as it helps you to recalibrate your life in the right order: God first and everything else follows. My cancer drove this point home for me. I needed to praise my husband and my praise for him came from a genuine place of love for him. I was so appreciative of every gesture of love, and I was so moved emotionally and spiritually by these gestures I felt I just had to tell him how grateful I was for everything he did, and also, I was just happy he was mine.

Our praise for God ought to come from the same place. Although I understood this point logically, it took a physical experience to really make this point come alive for me. We sing "Count your blessings, name them one by one," which highlights for me that our blessings are just too numerous to count. But now I believe true praise comes when we allow ourselves to be overwhelmed by the countless blessings of God, and that feeling of being overwhelmed results in praise. True praise occurs when you want to tell God how wonderful he is, not because He needs to hear it, but because you need to say it.

Praising God is like biofeedback for your soul, as it helps you to recalibrate your life in the right order: God first and everything else follows.

We have a choice when trials come - to focus on the trial or focus on the one who can carry you through the trial. Circumstances vary and can range from a late utility bill, to lost employment, to family discord, to chronic illness, all the way to death. Whatever the situation, no matter how big or how small, you have an opportunity to worry about the situation or focus on the joy and peace offered to you when you keep your mind directed toward God. Counting your blessings keeps you in the right frame of mind because your blessings are endless, and your current trial is temporary.

That is why we never give up. Though our bodies are dying, our spirits are being renewed every day. For our present troubles are small and won't last very long. Yet they produce for us a glory that vastly outweighs them and will last forever! So we don't look at the troubles we can see now; rather, we fix our gaze on things that cannot be seen. For the things we see now will soon be gone, but the things we cannot see will last forever. 2 Corinthians 4:16-18 (NLT).

This passage says our troubles produce a spiritual glory that far outweighs and outlasts our troubles. Every day we need to renew our mind, recalibrate it to focus on the things we cannot see but will last forever. Our salvation is forever. Our relationship with God is forever. Our peace is forever, and our blessings are forever. No one and no earthly circumstance can take these things from you. You, however, can give them away when you choose to keep your mind focused on your circumstances.

I was intent on not giving up any blessings God had prepared for me. I found another astounding blessing in a very negative circumstance. Two weeks after I was diagnosed with cancer, my daughter-in-law called to tell me her mother, Heather, was diagnosed with breast cancer. Again, I felt the kick in my stomach, the worry lines appeared, and the words "Oh no!" rushed out.

Counting your blessings keeps you in the right frame of mind because your blessings are endless, and your current trial is temporary.

From the time we met, Heather and I got along very well and I told her we are more than friends but sisters. I was devastated to hear this news about her diagnosis. I was worried, not for me or for Heather, but for my son and daughter-in-law because both mothers were now battling cancer. But this very unfortunate event became a blessing. Heather and I became cancer buddies. We compared notes often and shared information with each other from our doctors and oncology teams. We spoke often and encouraged each other through our different but similar journeys. We were miles apart on opposite coasts but that did not matter. We became close friends because no one really understood at the moment what we were going through but us. I never knew I needed a cancer buddy, but I am so very thankful God saw fit for us to be in each other's lives at this moment in time to support each other through these circumstances. *Thank you, God, for the lesson and the blessing.*

Again, we have a choice to allow our circumstances to separate us from God or we can use our circumstances to draw closer to Him.

Can anything ever separate us from Christ's love? Does it mean He no longer loves us if we have trouble or calamity, or are persecuted, or hungry, or destitute, or in danger, or threatened with death? (As the scriptures say, "For your sake we are killed every day; we are being slaughtered like sheep."). No, despite all these things, overwhelming victory is ours through Christ, who loved us. And I am convinced that nothing can ever separate us from God's love. Neither death nor life, neither angels nor demons, neither our fears for today nor our worries about tomorrow–not even the powers of hell can separate us from God's love. No power in the sky above or in the earth below–indeed, nothing in all creation will ever be able to separate us from the love of God that is revealed in Christ Jesus our Lord. Romans 8:35-39 (NLT).

Your Lessons Learned

1. Consider your life. What blessings has God provided that you have not given Him praise for?

____

____

____

____

2. When you think of your struggles, can you also think of a worse situation than yours? How can you change your current situation into an opportunity to praise God?

____

____

____

____

3. How can you make your foundation for life more focused on God and less focused on self?

____

____

____

____

Four

The Battle

This is what the Lord says, "Tell the whole world, and keep nothing back. Raise a signal flag to tell everyone that Babylon will fall!" Jeremiah 50:2 (NLT).

When I received my diagnosis, I began to prepare myself for battle. I viewed my cancer as the enemy, and I had to get ready to fight this enemy. I even did a whole photo shoot dressed like the female warriors in the movie "Black Panther." That was fun!

I prepared my army of soldiers by assigning tasks to loved ones. My sister was in charge of low sugar desserts because sugar feeds cancer, and I love sugar. My kids were the laugh squad, and my eldest daughter was my driver. My husband was my second in command throughout the entire battle. I made plaques that said, "God is my Protector," and my niece made me a cup that said, "Babylon Will Fall." Yet, in all of this preparation, nothing could take away the fear crouched behind every breath because no one can really prepare you for the unknown. That is the worst part of any battle, not knowing how it will end.

Will I win or will I lose?

Will I live or will I die?

What will chemotherapy feel like?

Will I be extremely ill or just uncomfortable?

Will I be able to enjoy life, or will I be bedridden the entire time?

Will there be permanent symptoms I will have to contend with for the rest of my life, or will I bounce back to my prior level of activity?

Fear of the unknown is the biggest enemy to battle. But there were other battles ahead also: the battle to keep my sense of humor, the battle to not slip into a depression, the battle to maintain a positive and hopeful attitude. I knew I was entering the biggest and most difficult wrestling ring I had ever encountered, and I was not able to tap out. There was no one who could take my place or help carry the load.

When it is obvious we cannot win this battle with our own resources, we have no option but to turn to God and beg Him for His assistance.

No one in my wonderful support system could sit in the chemotherapy chair for me. There were parts of this battle I had to fight alone. In all my battle preparations, I was trying to strengthen my resolve to enter the battle. I wanted to walk through those clinic doors with an air of determination that *this would not break me*. I believe I accomplished this, but fear was always present because there were new symptoms and surprises with every treatment. Even if I was able to walk through those doors physically, how could I keep my spirit from crumbling into a ball of nerves, or from being overtaken with depression? I am so thankful for my faith which is always waiting for me to give me moments of hope and reminders that the God I serve is the most powerful of all. I found comfort in God because He is my ever-present help. No matter what time of day or where I am, I can always say, "Lord, I need you right now."

The Lord reminded me He already prepared me for this battle. God never sends us into battle without our armor. The Bible is filled with examples of battles won by the power of the Lord, while the soldiers were just the conduits of God's power. I knew I could not win this battle without the Lord. I thought of the account of Gideon when God told him before a battle the army he recruited was too large.

The Lord said to Gideon, "You have too many warriors with you. If I let all of you fight the Midianites, the Israelites will boast to me that they saved themselves by their own strength." Judges 7:2 (NLT).

The army started with 32,000 men before God told Gideon to reduce that number and only 10,000 men remained. God told Gideon he still had too many men, and by the end of the selection process the army had dwindled to 300 men. A 32,000-man army sounds great to me, but an army of just 300 men seems like an impossible feat for Gideon, and a definite death sentence. And that is what God wants us to recognize. For Gideon alone, it was impossible. When it is obvious we cannot win this battle with our own resources, we have no option but to turn to God and beg Him for His assistance. After God dwindled the army to three hundred men, he allowed Gideon to go and scope out the Midianite army.

The armies of Midian, Amalek, and the people of the east had settled in the valley like a swarm of locusts. Their camels were like grains of sand on the seashore—too many to count! Judges 7:12 (NLT).

I wonder what Gideon thought when he looked at the Midianite army then looked at his army of only three hundred. God allowed Gideon to receive a prophecy that indicated Gideon and his army would win, and this greatly strengthened Gideon's bravery to march into battle with this tiny army.

God strengthened me also by reminding me He prepared me too for this battle. Cancer is a devastating diagnosis to receive and to many it is a death sentence. But because I am a child of God, after the initial shock and worry calmed down some, I took the opportunity to look for God's presence in this battle. When I looked for Him, I understood even if the doctor were to say, "Stage four and you only have six months to live," nothing was impossible with God. I know with God I will either receive life now or I will receive death with the promise of eternal life later.

As a child of God both are acceptable responses if we are able to have a Christ-like mind and say, "Not my will but thine Lord." Just like Jesus who prayed vehemently he would not have to walk down his path toward crucifixion, I vehemently did not want to walk this path of cancer. But also, like Jesus, I had to get to the point where I accepted this is my journey now and say, "Not my will but thine." It is in those moments when you have nothing left and you have to accept you must walk that path, even while every fiber of your being is crying, "I do not want to do this!"

Then God reminds you, "You are not alone, my child."

I realize to some these words may sound empty. How will acknowledging I am God's child help me with what I am facing? How will acknowledging God even exists help me? Many might say, "I am strong enough and I don't need anyone or anything to help me." And you may be right. Physically you might be strong enough to handle whatever this life may bring. The challenge is when we expend all the mental fortitude necessary for so many of life's battles, we are often left angry, tired, and disillusioned about life in general. It is in those moments you have an opportunity to stay angry and tired or choose to consider another outcome.

With God you have the opportunity of a different outcome. In those times when I could not sleep and the whole house was quiet I could either bemoan my situation or pray and sing praises to God. This I believe is a tool God gives us to allow us to depend on Him and experience His power as we slowly turn our focus from our situation to God's power to heal, to soothe, and to provide. God became more than a higher power I prayed to; He was the one holding my hand through the journey. In fact, in times of deep trouble, it may be necessary to stay in a constant state of prayer and worship to the Lord because anything outside of God will not help move your spirit from despair to hope.

God always provides you with what you need to make it through the journey He has allowed you to be on.

God always provides you with what you need to make it through the journey He has allowed you to be on. Often, what I needed was reassurance I was going to be all right. I found comfort believing whatever the outcome, God was in control. He is the best general there is, perfect at making sure we are equipped for the challenges and battles to come. Sometimes we don't use the equipment He provides us, but it is always there, ready for us to utilize. Even when we can't see a way out, God has already provided it. Sometimes, what we thought was a decision of our own will, was actually God preparing us for the battle to come.

For example, four years ago, I decided to try vegetarianism because with my age came a slower digestive system that led to all sorts of unmentionable complications. When I started cutting out meat from my diet, I did not intend for it to be a lifelong change, but it just came naturally. After four years I am what my daughter calls a "Flexitarian," meaning I mostly eat like a vegetarian, but if the mood hits me, I may eat a steak, fish, or a turkey burger. I did not know when I decided to be a vegetarian/pescatarian that this diet is recommended for cancer patients. I found myself in a position where I thought I was in charge of my life and my choices were just that - mine. How could I have known when I started changing my diet it would turn out to be one of the weapons I would need going through this Cancer battle? Looking back, I can see God's hand preparing me for this battle. I thought I was choosing but I believe God led me to this for my benefit.

This example and many other things I experienced were God making His presence known during my battle. While I was simply doing all I could down here, He was orchestrating far above and beyond my own vision. I believe our previous and current trials are building blocks to help with whatever the next challenge may be, and there will be more challenges. Decisions you believe you are independently making are really God training you and leading you to the knowledge and experiences He wants you to have.

Take a look at your past struggles, see how they might apply to what you are going through today, and ask yourself, "What did I learn during that trial that will help me get through this one with a smile on my face, and joy in my heart?"

The first thing that comes to my mind is, "I made it through that trial, so I know I can make it through this one." Each trial I face and complete further proves to me God is by my side because I still have hope. Hope makes the next trial not necessarily easier, but a bit less heavy with Him shouldering the load.

For instance, it has taken me a long time to call myself a teacher, and I know that this spiritual gift was cultivated by the Lord even when

I thought I was making the decisions. I remember my first teaching experience was for purely selfish reasons, but God used that first experience as a building block toward the plans He had for my life.

When I was sixteen, I attended a Bible study class with a teacher who had a very strong southern accent and a particular drawl that made words sound very strange to me. On one occasion the teacher said the word, "appendages" but it sounded like, "appenges." My teenage-self had little control over my mouth, and I blurted out, "ap-pen-dages!" That was the last time I attended that class deciding then and there I could not sit through this class with this teacher without getting myself into serious trouble.

Instead, I volunteered to assist teaching the nursery school class. I was not interested in teaching at all, I just wanted to get out of the class so I could save myself from further outbursts and from my mother's discipline and look of disappointment when the teacher reported my behavior to her. I never went back to that class, and I accidentally stumbled onto something I found myself enjoying. I had selfish motives for teaching that nursery class, but God used it to prepare me for what He wanted me to do. To God be the glory for His omniscience.

I believe our previous and current trials are building blocks to help with whatever the next challenge may be, and there will be more challenges.

I felt so content and at peace every time I acknowledged God's presence and His active participation in leading my life and this battle. But God does not only show up like this in battle. He is *always* present and constantly an active participant in our lives. Being able to see God in our storm is a great weapon God has provided us during any battle.

Often the problem is we are wearing the wrong glasses to see God. These are not glasses you can pick up at the local drugstore. These glasses are formed as you grow in your relationship with him. If you do not know God, then you do not have these glasses and you will not see God. The person who introduces you to God, has your glasses. If you are a Christian but you are not seeking God, then your prescription is old, and you will not find God.

Believing in Jesus is only the beginning of our Christian journey. The work begins after we have made the commitment to follow Christ and part of that work is actively seeking God. God is always present, but it is only through consistent study, prayer, fellowship with other believers, and living a faithful obedient life that you see Him clearly. As we live our lives and focus on spiritual things, God becomes more and more clear, as if our lens prescription changes as we grow closer and closer to him. But what about those times when we are unable to study, pray, or fellowship with others? What about those times when I was too nauseous and could not focus on my husband's words, much less, on the words in the Bible? In those moments, I rested in the fact God knew my heart, and my desire to commune with Him even if I was physically unable to.

I am so thankful God offers us opportunities to grow and with that growth the prescription of my spiritual glasses changes so I can see Him more and more in my life.

You know when you get your eyes checked and they change the lenses then ask you, "Which is better, one or two?" The Bible is the optometrist helping us correct our vision of God. If you are not in the word your glasses will not improve. Even in a raging battle that is taxing, devastating, and wears us down, we can and should be prioritizing our vision and relationship with God. There are so many struggles and troubles that afflict all of us. It might be cancer, an overbearing boss, a strained relationship with your family, marital issues, or even navigating the challenges of depression. With all of the things that can obscure our spiritual vision, it is critical we do our best to gain clarity to see God so we can manage and navigate whatever we come across in the world.

Decisions you believe you are independently making are really God training you and leading you to the knowledge and experiences He wants you to have.

It may not always be easy to consistently prioritize our relationship with God, but I have found it always comes down to the choices we make. It became clearer to me during this journey that we have a choice in every situation to look for God, find God, and allow God to take the helm. I reject the idea I have to fight for anything, instead choosing to let God fight my battles for me. When I expressed frustration to others, they would say to me, "You have to advocate for yourself." I thought over and over again, but Jesus is my advocate.

There were times I wanted to fight so badly to get information, when I was so frustrated with either the medical system, my doctors, or the nurses that all I wanted to do was go and get the answers myself. However, in some of those moments of frustration when I tried to call for answers and bend the system to make it answer to my will, the response I always got was I must wait. It took some time and some failures, but eventually I came to another realization I am not actually waiting on the system: *I am waiting on God.*

This point came crashing home one afternoon when I was so fed up and tired of waiting for information I picked up the phone to call the nurse to demand answers. While I was on hold with the medical office, all of a sudden, the other line rang, and the nurse I was trying to call was actually calling me. God's timing is perfect, and there is nothing you or I can do to change that perfect plan.

"What did I learn during the trial that will help me get through this one with a smile on my face, and joy in my heart?"

One of the more difficult things that became clearer to me about God's plan is I also learned not to jump to conclusions. Early on in the process, I received the results of my first CT scan through my patient portal on a Friday which to my untrained eye showed some unusual growths. My mind immediately went to more cancer, and my heart raced. I worried about the possibility I may have more cancer. But since I did not know for sure, I chose not to say anything to anyone, not even to Ernie, until I heard from the doctor. Patience is also a tool to use during battles. It was a nerve-racking weekend again, and I involved myself with busy work to distract my mind. I had to wait until the following Tuesday to hear the doctor say no cancer anywhere other than the uterus. I was informed that the abnormalities I read in the report are common abnormalities that do not indicate cancer. I was so thankful I did not overreact and begin to fret. Instead of fretting, the thought that kept rising to the surface was: *even if it is more cancer, God is able.*

The same day we celebrated the results of that CT scan, we also got a call from the finance department stating there were issues and conflicts with the two insurances we were using. I was frustrated again, and my joy from the CT scan quickly faded as I tried to bolster my spirit to now deal with another roadblock. Whoever thought having two insurances would be a problem? My immediate reaction was panic, but eventually I was able to use the weapon of prayer, and I prayed, "Lord, You got this. Lord, You have brought me this far and You will take care of this, too. Lord, You are moving mountains for me, and You will move this one. Lord, please fix this as I am Your child. In Jesus name, amen."

"For I know the plans I have for you," says the Lord. "They are plans for good and not for disaster, to give you a future and a hope." Jeremiah 29:1 (NLT).

As I pondered this verse, I considered that physical ailments are not our greatest battle. The plans God has for us are for us to prosper spiritually. The spiritual battle is far more important than the physical battle because the result of our spiritual battle determines our final resting place. Neither our financial health nor our physical health has any bearing on our eternal home, only our spiritual health. However, our spirituality can greatly affect our finances and our health as we depend on Christ to develop Godly characteristics in us that are beneficial to all areas of our lives.

Godly characteristics are paramount, but they will not stop nature. Because our bodies are flesh and blood, we are all susceptible to any failures, defects, diseases, or disabilities that may afflict flesh and blood. It is certain that we all will experience a decline in our physical health as we age if God blesses us to live. Even when we accept that our bodies are not perfect, and we accept physical decline as normal there are opportunities to praise God through the uncertainties of what that decline will look like for each of us.

For we are not fighting against flesh and blood enemies but against evil rulers and authorities of the unseen world, against mighty powers in this dark world, and against evil spirits in the heavenly places. Ephesians 6:12 (NLT).

This verse makes more sense to me now, too. Since I was facing the most difficult physical battle of my life, I was forced to consider what was really important. The most important battle is not physical to defend flesh, but the battle of most importance is against Satan who is battling to win our soul from God. The only way to win this battle is to stand firm on the word of God, and to allow God's word to permeate every aspect of our lives. Allow God's word to guide us through all other battles knowing God is fighting Satan constantly to keep our soul out of his grasp. Our battle is to keep our mind, our focus, our actions, our thoughts, our will, and our purpose solidly planted in the word of God. In those midnight contemplations I rested in the belief that if this body fails, I know my spirit is safe in the Lord. Even as I prayed for physical healing, my spirit could be at peace because I have an eternal home waiting for me.

Our battle is to keep our mind, our focus, our actions, our thoughts, our will, and our purpose solidly planted in the word of God.

This is why the most important weapons we have at our disposal are the weapons that keep us connected to God.

Therefore, put on every piece of God's armor so you will be able to resist the enemy in the time of evil. Then after the battle you will still be standing firm. Stand your ground, putting on the belt of truth and the body armor of God's righteousness. For shoes, put on the peace that comes from the Good News so you will be fully prepared. In addition to all of these, hold up the shield of faith to stop the fiery arrows of the devil. Put on salvation as your helmet, and take the sword of the Spirit, which is the word of God. Praying always with all prayer and supplication in the Spirit and watching thereunto with all perseverance and supplication for all saints. Ephesians 6:13-18 (NLT).

These are the most important weapons and the only weapons that will help me to defeat Satan in his battle to win my soul. These weapons keep me protected from Satan by keeping God as the priority in my life. Without this focus God will not win the battle for my soul, but Satan will. Focusing on these spiritual weapons will keep our minds and souls safe in the hands of the Lord, and away from the schemes of the devil. These weapons are important when going through battles because Satan is looking for any opportunity to put doubt in our minds. With these weapons, we can keep our minds focused on hope and salvation where Satan cannot touch us.

Satan hoped to break my spirit with cancer, but God used it to strengthen me. Satan tried and was successful at times to keep my mind on the "what ifs."

What if I do have stage four cancer?

What if I survive cancer but am left disabled in some way?

What if I cannot return to work?

What if I am left too weak to do the things I once enjoyed?

These were real fears and with the small urges from the Holy Spirit I was able to turn my gaze away from the physical and focus on the possibility God had a better plan, which included growing in wisdom from the current circumstances.

Your Lessons Learned

1. What did I learn during a trial that will help me get through the next one with a smile on my face, and joy in my heart?

____

____

____

____

2. If your biggest fear came to fruition, what would be the end result for your soul?

____

____

____

____

3. How can you prepare for your biggest fear?

____

____

____

____

Five

The Hair

How beautiful you are, my darling! Oh, how beautiful! Your eyes behind your veil are doves. Your hair is like a flock of goats descending from Mount Gilead. Song of Solomon 4:1. (NLT).

The educational package I received about my particular chemotherapy medication told me I would lose my hair. The reality of that fact did not really hit me until later. Until then I decided to play with the hair I had for as long as I had it.. The first great idea was to dye it blonde. I have always wanted to know what I would look like as a blonde, and surprisingly, I loved it!

My daughters, Camile and Rachel, and I planned an all-girls weekend before my surgery and treatment.. This was the perfect time to dye my hair. Rachel dyed my hair and then both girls did a full photo shoot of me dressed like the female African warriors in the movie, *Wakanda*. This was very entertaining. It was also fun to shock my husband. After a month as a blonde, I decided to really shock him, and dyed it bright red.

He walked in my office to greet me after returning home for the day, and the look of horror on his face was priceless. His mouth froze open, and his eyes bugged out. He then slapped his hand to his mouth and mumbled as he turned and bolted from the room. I can only imagine the curse words that were being said behind that hand. One week before my first chemotherapy treatment, it was time to get serious and I dyed it a normal shade of brown. I was beginning the preparation for battle.

I was informed that my hair would begin to fall out within two weeks after the first treatment. Like clockwork my scalp started to tingle ten days after my first chemotherapy treatment. I held on for as long as I could before the tingling turned to tenderness and I began taking medication to dull the pain. As I combed my hair, I noticed more hair in the comb. If I pulled on a lock of hair, it would come out in my hand. After the second treatment I decided it was time to shave it off. This was not an easy decision as I had never seen myself bald before.

If you are dealing with life issues, thank God you are alive to deal with these issues, whatever they may be.

I wore a short curly style I loved, and I received compliments often about my natural curly hair. I considered the cold cap therapy which is a treatment that freezes your scalp during chemotherapy so that the drugs will not enter your hair follicles. It is reported to work but the thought of sitting for four to five hours with a freezing scalp did not appeal to me. I tried to wear the ice gloves and socks that were supposed to reduce the possibility of neuropathy, and it worked for several patients. The socks were not so bad, but my hands hurt terribly as they approached freezing, and when I decided I could not handle that feeling, I felt more pain when my hands began to warm up again. I decided this was too much and I would deal with whatever may come. Unfortunately, I did experience the neuropathy in my hands and feet and that pain made me cry too. Thankfully, it was temporary, and all the pain eventually disappeared. I know I was blessed because many cancer patients suffer from permanent neuropathy after their cancer treatments are complete.

I also resolved that baldness was just a side effect I had to deal with, and I knew my hair would eventually grow back. I asked my husband to shave my head and invited my girls to be my support. My daughters gathered around me and played India Arie's song, "I Am Not My Hair." We danced around, laughed, and hugged before the clippers came out. I could not look while my husband shaved my head, and the tears began to flow.

The tears were not because I was losing my hair, but because I was angry at cancer for making me do this. Everything I had experienced because of cancer to this point came pouring out in those tears. I was angry due to the diagnosis, and the subsequent surgery. I was angry I had to take a leave of absence due to the surgery, then five more days with every treatment. I cried because I was putting my family through this with me, yet so appreciative of their presence. When my husband was finished, he hugged and kissed me and told me I was beautiful. I did not believe him. Immediately, the pain in my scalp stopped, and I knew I had made the right decision. My daughter, Rachel, the photographer, again suggested a photo shoot right then and there. I put on my African necklace and had a look on my face that said, "Cancer you picked the wrong Lady to mess with!"

Over time, my eyebrows and eyelashes also fell out and I finally had to admit I looked like a cancer patient. There was no hiding from it, and I now had to reevaluate what I considered beautiful. I did not want to hide, but I also did not want people staring at me. I considered wigs but I have never worn wigs before, and I did not want to invest in something I hoped I would not need for very long, so, I went the headwrap route. I got used to my bald head very quickly, and only wore wraps to avoid stares or comments.

Once I went bald to an oncology appointment, and a nurse stared at me from the time I entered the nursing station area until I entered my assigned examination room. I thought, *what the heck!* You should be used to seeing bald heads here! She did not boost my confidence about being seen bald, and I did not do that again. But honestly, when I saw another female with a bald head my thought was always *she is brave and she is rocking that bald head.* Still, I usually wore my headwrap when I went out, especially at church because I did not want to be a distraction.

In an effort to not let baldness depress me I began taking pictures with every bald man in my life and it became my little game on my hair journey. My husband wanted to shave his head in solidarity, but I would not let him. My reasoning was that every time I looked at him with his bald head, it would only remind me I had cancer, and I did not want that. I wanted him and everyone around me to look normal and go about their normal lives to remind me that a normal life was waiting for me when this was all over.

I noticed I did not look in the mirror much anymore since there was nothing to admire or fix. I realized I would continue this journey without any concern for my looks. This was not too traumatic for me because I have always been a low maintenance woman. I do not get my hair done in a beauty parlor because in my mind there is always something more exciting to do than sit for hours in a beauty salon. I learned to cut my own hair, and I wore minimal make up. I love the look of a well-made face, but I lack the patience it takes to get it. I did not wear acrylic nails except for special occasions, again because I did not want to commit to waiting in the nail salon for fills every three weeks. I got pedicures because the schedule was when I wanted to go, and if I waited six weeks, no one would know the difference. Although having a bald head was traumatic, it was not as traumatic as it could have been if I was someone who prided themselves on perfect beauty every day.

Thankfully, my cancer journey was during the Covid pandemic so my work as a field social worker was completely telephonic thus no need to get dressed up or made up.

In a way, not having the daily concerns of beauty was freeing. It allowed me time to focus on other areas of my character that had nothing to do with outward appearance. Scripture tells us:

But the Lord said to Samuel, "... The Lord doesn't see things the way you see them. People judge by outward appearance, but the Lord looks at the heart." 1 Samuel 16:7 (NLT).

This was my lesson. If God looks at the heart, we should also spend more time evaluating our heart and considering the hearts of others without the influence of their appearance. Without the distraction of outer beauty and all the contraptions that go with it we have a better opportunity to know someone on a deeper level. It is really difficult to separate our physical image from our spiritual. So much of who we are and what we do is intertwined with how we look.

We ought to evaluate what people are attracted to when they see us. Are we putting more effort into looking a certain way than in behaving a certain way?

I am constantly on some form of a meal plan and always exercising because of an image I have in my mind I want to achieve. I tell myself I am working hard on myself because I want to be healthy and keep this body running at its best so I can work for as long as I can for the Lord. This is true, but honestly the first motivation is because I want to look good, and I enjoy feeling good and looking good. I have colored my hair in the past because I did not want the gray hair to show my age.

However, at this moment any hair, no matter what color, would have been more welcome than this bald head.

Circumstances forced me to reconsider my views on appearance and ask, what is more important than how I look? I think this is an important question for everyone to ask as it appears that society is more concerned with one's outer appearance than with inner character. I am surprised at all the selfies people take on their phones, including me, and the large amounts of money people spend on a single piece of clothing or accessory because they want the latest trend.

I am perplexed by others who after they say hello always say something about the other person's appearance. I would love to say to myself it is because I'm fabulous, but the truth is society has us all trained to focus on external beauty. Still, I yearn for more meaningful conversations beyond what one is wearing. I experimented a few times by asking people after worship things like:

"What point resonated with you from the sermon today?"

"What are you studying in your personal devotions?"

"Do you have a prayer request you would like me to pray for?"

Not surprisingly people started avoiding me, so I stopped. Still, the desire for deeper spiritual topics continues. So, I went deeper in myself and asked, what does the Bible say on the topic of beauty? The first scripture that always comes to mind when I consider beauty is:

My servant grew up in the Lord's presence like a tender green shoot, like a root in dry ground. There was nothing beautiful or majestic about his appearance, nothing to attract us to him. Isaiah 53:2 (NLT).

I love this prophesy about Jesus because it reminds us that people were not attracted to Jesus because of his outer beauty because Jesus was physically ugly. This is amazing because Jesus is the most prominent person in history, whose life touched and continues to change the lives of millions of people. If we are striving to be like Jesus, then our outer beauty must take a back seat to our spiritual beauty. We ought to evaluate what people are attracted to when they see us. Are we putting more effort into looking a certain way than in behaving a certain way?

Don't be concerned about the outward beauty of fancy hairstyles, expensive jewelry, or beautiful clothes. You should clothe yourselves instead with the beauty that comes from within, the unfading beauty of a gentle and quiet spirit, which is so precious to God. I Peter 3:3-4 (NLT).

I have heard the rebuttal to this passage that asks, "Should we then dress in plain, drab clothing and give no attention to our hair or face?" I do not believe this is what the passage teaches. I believe it teaches that we should be more concerned with inner beauty. If we are more concerned with how we look than the condition of our hearts, then God is not pleased.

Cancer reminded me that time is precious, and no one is promised tomorrow. Cancer forced me to consider how I wanted to be remembered if this was my time to die. I concluded I did not want to be remembered first for my looks or style of dress, but I wanted to be remembered for the love I displayed. I wanted my attempts to be helpful to others to speak for me. This requires one to ignore the societal pull toward shallowness, and the attempts of Satan to trick us into believing that what we look like is of utmost importance. This constant attention to outer beauty may also be rooted in a lack of self-love. The fact that many cannot look at themselves without constant criticism of a physical feature is an indication of insecurity, self-doubt, or low self-esteem. This passage freed me from that:

Thank You for making me so wonderfully complex! Your workmanship is marvelous - how well I know it. Psalm 139:14 (NLT).

I remember meditating on this verse for the first time and saying to myself, *if God says I am wonderful and marvelous, then I am wonderful and marvelous!* This freed me from trying to be anything other than who God intended for me to be. I no longer have to try to fit into some arbitrary societal mold that changes with the wind.

So, I am bald, I have no eyebrows or eyelashes, and everyone knows I am a cancer patient. What lessons may God want me to learn from this experience? At some point in our lives, we have to conclude that what other people think about us is not a motivation to do anything, because others will not speak for us on the day of judgment. What matters to God is what we do with the life He has given us to please Him.

At some point in our lives, we have to conclude that what other people think about us is not a motivation to do anything, because others will not speak for us on the day of judgment.

I am also learning that no matter how hard you try, there will always be someone who has an issue with you. This fact was very difficult for me to accept because I want everyone to like me, and when I learn that someone is not happy with me in some way, it affects me deeply. Most often, it is my mouth that has caused a riff and I have to live with the fact that I have unintentionally burned bridges. I admit I have "Foot in Mouth Disease" and I am in constant prayer God remove the foot and replace it with the ability to choose my words more carefully. Thankfully, God has answered this prayer, and I now have "Toe in Mouth Disease." I also accept that this is my thorn in the flesh to deal with and I am praying God's grace will cover my sins and allow me to enter heaven one day. So, I made the best of my bald head not concerned with what others thought of it.

This hair journey was weirdly exciting. I hated losing my hair but then I got obsessed with the journey to regrow it. After the fourth treatment, I began to see peach fuzz on my scalp and one lone gray hair popped up. I named him, "Harry the Hair." Two months later, Harry's twin sisters arrived, "Laverne and Shirley." I was amazed that as my hair began to grow, it was all gray and very straight. I daydreamed about being a silver fox and I was happy with that picture because gray hair is better than no hair.

The regrowth of my hair fascinated me as I watched it change from straight to curly, and gray to black. But it went deeper than that. Watching my hair grow was symbolic of watching my life grow into whatever new chapter God had in store for me because I was different after cancer. My priorities changed and I no longer wanted to be in the fast lane of life reaching for more bells and whistles of this world. I acknowledged God had blessed me with life, and I wanted whatever life I had left to be filled with love for God, for my family, for others, and the simple enjoyment of just being alive. I wanted more time to spend with others, more time to enjoy all of my hobbies, and more time to see the beauty of nature. I also acknowledged I was blessed to even consider this as an option.

I definitely felt a new sense of purpose after cancer. I became very aware of others who were battling cancer. It is strange how we do not notice things until it happens to us. I was not aware of how many people have been touched by cancer either directly or indirectly. I wanted to be a resource just to share my experiences in hopes that it would reduce someone's anxiety. I wanted to write this book with the hope that it would encourage someone who may be facing the same battle. I also developed a new point of view regarding life's issues. If you are dealing with life issues, thank God you are alive to deal with these issues, whatever they may be.

Your Lessons Learned

1. What is more important than how you look?

2. What are people attracted to when they see you?

3. How can you change your priorities if needed?

Figure 1

He said I was beautiful

Figure 2

Cancer You Picked The Wrong one!

Figure 3

Bald With Son Jared

Figure 4

I Look like a cancer patient

Six

The Bond

"By this shall all men know that ye are my disciples, if you have love one for another." John 13:35 (NLT).

What does it mean to serve one another? What does it mean to love another? We know that we should do these things, and we teach others often just by repeating these quotes and phrases. Service to others is something I thought I had a solid grasp on before I found myself being served by others in ways I couldn't have foreseen. There is only so much wisdom and knowledge that we truly absorb through academic pursuits, with the vast majority of wisdom being developed through the experiences that test our boundaries and expectations.

For example, I have historically been uncomfortable when consoling the bereaved. I felt lost and awkward while I looked for the right words or meaningful gestures to extend during a time of great loss. Simply put, I just did not know what to do or say. It felt like I was always on the outside looking in, like an unwanted guest at an event or gathering. Then, in 2010, my father passed away. I became the recipient of well-wishers and realized the wide spectrum of things that actually could be done to comfort the bereaved. These are things I would not have had the opportunity to learn about if I had not experienced it firsthand.

I did not know of the custom of giving money to the family of the deceased. Now I have been through it, this makes sense because I did not know all the costs associated with dying, funerals, closing someone's accounts, etcetera. One sister from church came with an entire meal for the family including drinks and dessert. Now it makes sense that when you are busy taking care of the business of someone's death, you often forget the simple things of life like cooking. My father's funeral was the first time I heard our elder say, "It's all in the bond." I understood immediately what he meant by that, and it was comforting. He meant that because we are family in Christ, the bond of family makes helping each other in times of need just part of what we do for each other.

The same is true for encouraging the ill. Cancer made me rethink how I respond to the sick. For many years I believed the appropriate response to the sick was to say a prayer and send a card. But how does someone pray for the sick? My approach was to customarily write down the names of all the sick people who requested prayer, then at home I would take my list out and call that name in prayer. My approach was to call that person's name in prayer, but is that really what it means to pray for the sick?

Does God need me to call out their name in prayer?

Will He forget if I don't call their name?

How is reading a list of names in prayer meaningful?

These are questions I asked myself now that I was the recipient of service from others. It caused me to look back at the support I was giving to those around me. Something that helped me answer these questions honestly is the foundational belief that everything God commands us to do is not for His benefit but for ours. So how does calling out a list of names in prayer benefit me or benefit the person I was praying for?

And the prayer of faith shall save the sick, and the Lord shall raise him up; and if he has committed sins, they shall be forgiven him. Confess your faults one to another and pray one for another that ye may be healed. The effectual fervent prayer of a righteous man availeth much. James 5:15-16 (KJV).

Matthew Henry's Commentary explains this best:

"And when a righteous person, a true believer, justified in Christ, and by his grace walking before God in holy obedience, presents an effectual fervent prayer, wrought in his heart by the power of the Holy Spirit, raising holy affections and believing expectations and so leading earnestly to plead the promises of God at his mercy-seat, it avails much. It is not enough to say a prayer, but we must pray in prayer. Thoughts must be fixed, desires must be firm and ardent, and graces exercised. This instance of the power of prayer, encourages every Christian to be earnest in prayer." [1]

This description of prayer looks very different from my list of names I recited. I recognized I needed to spend more time with each name and allow the Holy Spirit to guide me in prayer for this person. I needed to make each prayer, and each name, a personal and intimate part of my conversation with God. It is an act of service to pray for someone in this manner. My experiences started to make me ask questions like:

How do I want others to pray for me?

Do I want my name recited from a list, or do I want someone to spend time at the throne pleading for my healing?

1 Bible Hub. "James 5." Expositor's Bible Commentary. Accessed July 23, 2022, https://biblehub.com/commentaries/expositors/james/5.html.

It is obvious that everyone would prefer the latter. Praying for others in this manner is an act of sacrifice as it takes time to call each name and say more than, "Pray for John Smith." It takes time and thought to consider what specifically about John Smith should I pray for?

As I considered this, in addition to the immediate prayer request of healing, a job, travel, or peace in the home, I believe we have an opportunity to pray for a person's spiritual wellbeing as well. Now the playing field is broadened, and we have so many different ways to pray for John Smith. I thank God for opening my eyes to this lesson.

I recognized I needed to spend more time with each name and allow the Holy Spirit to guide me in prayer for this person. I needed to make each prayer, and each name, a personal and intimate part of my conversation with God.

My second approach for encouragement was to send greeting cards to those who were sick or bereaved. However, when I became the recipient of several greeting cards, I began to question the actual meaning behind them. When I open a greeting card my first thought is, *oh, how nice someone thought of me to send a card. Someone is thinking about me and wants to lift my spirits.* And I suppose if this is the primary goal of greeting cards, then mission accomplished. I just started to wonder if there could be a bigger impact than that?

When I get a card, I also look at it and think, *wow, they spent money on this.* I will display the cards I receive for a week or so, but eventually my cards end up in the trash. I apologize to everyone who has sent me cards if this offends you. I know there are some that hold on to all of their greeting cards forever, however, I am just not one of them. As I pondered this tradition of sending greeting cards, I wondered if there was more I could be doing. In this digital era phone calls are becoming obsolete and being replaced by a text message. But even today there is something special and personal about a phone call.

A phone call means you stopped what you were doing, took time out of your day, and chose to call me at that moment. Nothing can replace the human connection that occurs when we are face to face or voice to voice. Often, I will hear people say, "I thought about calling you, but I didn't want to bother you."

This statement always leaves me perplexed and the first question in my mind is, *well, do you like to receive phone calls?* Then I think, *how do you handle it when others call you and you are busy?* Don't we all feel joy knowing someone was thinking about us? Don't we all want someone else to feel that same joy? This point can really frustrate me because there are people I will call, and we have a seemingly great conversation. Yet, that same person will never call me. I will get into my feelings and start the passive aggressive cycle by saying, "I am not calling them again until they call me." The challenge I have with that line of thinking is that without fail the Holy Spirit will put them on my mind over and over again until I give in and call.

I have to stay consciously and constantly spiritual on this topic because my carnal side wants to shut the door on many. In those moments, my spiritual side says, "Marcia do what is right and God will take care of the rest." Yet, I am human, and I must battle with myself not to let the carnal win.

I encourage those of you who may be reluctant to call others to do just that instead of waiting for someone to call you. I encourage you to pick up the phone and touch someone's life with your voice. I understand the fear of rejection may hinder you somewhat but try to focus on why you are calling. Allow the love behind the why to outweigh the fear of rejection. However, from my experience of randomly calling people, I have never been rejected. Instead, I am usually greeted with a very warm, "Hello."

Hello goes a very long way for someone who is not feeling well. Cancer made me ask myself, *am I really serving others by mentioning them in prayer and sending a get-well card? Could I be doing more?* I believe if you are physically or financially unable to do more, then these acts of service are very well accepted by God. But for me and others who can do more, I believe that we should. The question becomes, *what are you really sacrificing by mentioning a name in prayer and sending a card? Is this a service or is this an act of obligation to pray a name and send a card?*

These thoughts arose for me after I received acts of service, and love acts that truly touched my heart. My first love act came from Patty who had been diagnosed with breast cancer in the past. She arrived at my house with "A Box of Blessings" which were daily words of encouragement, a cup that said, "Cancer You Picked the Wrong Lady," and a mask that read, "I can do all things through Christ who strengthens me." I thought of the time and money she sacrificed for me and I was touched.

Then Alexa, a friend from church, sent a blanket with hearts on it, and her husband, Kevin, sent me a shirt that said, "God's Got This." The blanket became my chemotherapy blanket and I thought of her every time I used it. Another friend from church, Kathy, would come and sit with me for hours. Even though I felt a twinge of guilt she was taking this time away from her life, I was touched by her outpouring of love for me.

We can all think about ourselves and be selfish, but to be on the receiving end of selflessness is to truly feel love.

Charlotte knew I loved to sing praise songs, so she organized a praise night at my house with both of our families. I thoroughly enjoyed this evening and felt so blessed that everyone sacrificed their time to spend it with me singing praises. Finally, Charity bought me a staff and she attached a note to it that said, "Like Moses, when you find yourself in a battle you know you are ill-equipped to handle.... Remember just like Aaron and Hur held up Moses, our prayers will hold you up." I received plants, cookies, and fruit as well as phone calls, text messages, and greeting cards. Every gift and gesture brought a smile to my face and the warm, cozy feeling that comes from knowing you are loved.

These gestures highlighted for me I could be doing a lot more than a prayer and a greeting card for other people in my life. What struck me the most and made these acts of love so special was not the money spent but the time spent. I could buy for myself any gift that was given but the thought behind the gesture is what was so special, and what no one can replicate for themselves. We can all think about ourselves and be selfish, but to be on the receiving end of selflessness is to truly feel love. I realized I was taking the easy way out with a prayer and a card, and there really was no sacrifice in my efforts. I vowed to be more sacrificial in my service to others.

If someone has enough money to live well and sees a brother or sister in need but shows no compassion—how can God's love be in that person? Dear children, let's not merely say that we love each other; let us show the truth by our actions. 1 John 3:17-18 (NLT).

Again, I believe that true love of our brothers and sisters will be seen in our willingness to sacrifice for each other. The sacrifice will look different for each of us.

What I found to be the most important and the most meaningful aspect of service from others is that their acts of love remind me I have not been forgotten.

After my own experiences with chemotherapy, I felt compelled to apologize to my sister-in-law who was diagnosed with cancer years ago, and I realized I had not been very supportive of her at all. Of course, I prayed for her but that was the extent of it. I rationalized in my mind she had grown children, a husband, and sisters who were there to care for her, and so she did not need anything from me. But now I have been through the same journey, I realize I could have done so much better.

What I found to be the most important and the most meaningful aspect of service from others is that their acts of love reminded me I had not been forgotten. There are so many challenges that are attached to a serious medical condition from fear, to anxiety, stress, and anger. It can be difficult to understand the dynamics those feelings present without having gone through it. When you are on the outside looking in and you have never been through a serious illness, all you can do is try and have empathy and say to yourself, *that must be tough what they are going through.* However, now I have been through it, I can be much more sympathetic to others who are experiencing it. I can relate to the nausea, fatigue, neuropathy, bone pain, dizziness, and countless other symptoms and struggles that come from chemotherapy because I have personally experienced them. I can share my experiences and listen to their frustrations with patience because I have had the same frustrations. I hope I will be quick to reach out to others experiencing similar situations.

So many people say, "Call me if you need me." This statement falls flat for me even though I have also uttered it. When I hear this my carnal mind starts turning to thoughts like:

What would make me call you, especially if we have never had a relationship before now?

Have we ever talked on the phone before?

Why would we realistically start now?

Through my personal growth and maturity my advice is this: if you really want to be helpful and supportive to someone, then try to spend some time with them developing a relationship.

The few times I did call for help, it was to those I already had a relationship with. I called those who kept calling and repeating, "Call me for anything." Their consistency spoke to their authenticity, I believed they meant it, and that is what made me comfortable to call on them. It was not to the person who made the commonplace saying of, "Call me if you need me," and then I never heard from them again.

I wonder about the authenticity of people who continually use that phrase. Even now I look back and wonder what I thought would happen if someone actually did call me when I said it. A friend of mine said, "Call me even if you want something from the store." Internally I thought, *I already have people around me who do that for me.*

Another friend said, "Call even if you just want to talk." Once again, my internal voice questioned how that conversation would go. If we have never really talked before or reached out to each other before this, the chances of me doing it now were very slim.

I started to play the conversation in my head if I were to call and reached the same conclusion each time. *I know what you are going to say so no need to call.* So, then the question presents itself as how should someone proceed who truly does want to be helpful even if there might not be an established relationship there? From my experience, if you want to be helpful, just find something to do for the person and do it. Even if you cannot think of a need they may have, just do something that shows you care or you were thinking about them.

Our expressions of love should not be dependent on how the other responds.

Another friend, Daniel, would randomly stop by with two Starbucks coffees in his hand. This love act shows a sincere desire to be helpful in a small way. But this is not small to me. This brother had to stop what he was doing, go to the coffee shop, choose what he thinks we might like, pay for the drinks, then drive to our house to deliver them. This is huge in my mind. In fact, every love act is huge to me and every act served its purpose, to remind me I am loved.

Also, remember that consistency is closely related to authenticity; don't just text once, or call once, or pray once. Continue reaching out. Those little gestures mean so much when you are going through difficult times. They mean so much when you can't leave your house or are in pain every time you walk to the bathroom or find yourself angry at the world. Even if they don't respond, do your best to continue to show some love anyway. Our expressions of love should not be dependent on how the other responds. Just like my random calls on the phone should not be dependent on if they will ever call me back. Remember the purpose of reaching out is to let someone know they are not alone, they are loved, and they are not forgotten. No one can really go through someone else's storm but consider what you can do to make the waves a little easier.

Can you drop off a meal for them?

Can you take their kids for the day?

Can you pay a utility bill for them?

Can you sing a song or read a scripture?

Can you send an encouraging text?

The most important thing is to let the people you are trying to support know they are loved and not forgotten. This is an integral part of our Christian journey. This love shown to others is exactly what scripture is referring to when it says,

By this shall all men know that ye are my disciples, if ye have love one to another. John 13:35 (KJV).

In fact, our acts of love define our Christianity because God is love. Good people in the world know how to do good deeds. But as a Christian our deeds are not rooted in a personal desire to help, but in our relationship with the one who is love. In our efforts to please God, if we are not actively seeking opportunities to show love to others, then we are not pleasing God.

Whatever your trouble is, God has allowed it because there are lessons He wants you to learn from your trouble.

Your Lessons Learned

1. What ways do you enjoy receiving love?

____

____

____

____

2. What opportunities may you have to grow in your service to others?

____

____

____

____

3. How can you decrease selfishness and increase selflessness?

____

____

____

____

Seven

The Attitude

Don't copy the behavior and customs of this world, but let God transform you into a new person by changing the way you think. Then you will learn to know God's will for you, which is good and pleasing and perfect. Romans 12:2 (NLT).

I was confused for a while when people were constantly telling me how strong I was for going through my cancer journey. My first thought was hello! I did not have a choice, guys. Once a trial is here, you cannot choose to not go through it. As a young Christian, I had the same thoughts of confusion when people would say about their own struggles, "I could not have made it without Jesus."

What do you mean you could not have made it?

Do you mean you would have died, or you would have failed somehow in going through your struggle?

Because no matter what, you have no choice but to make it through your trials. You cannot take a pass or get an excused absence when a trial begins in your life. You have no choice but to go through it. As I thought more about this, I understood that people were referring to the way and the attitude with which I was going through this current situation.

The only thing we have control over is how we will go through something, not always what we go through. As trials come at us, and they will come, again and again, will we maintain fear and dread in our heart, or will we maintain hope and joy? Having an intimate relationship with Christ significantly improves the possibility of going through trouble and ending up on the other side better than when you started. I know from firsthand experience how difficult this concept can be to fully accept, especially when the trials at hand are daunting, unbearable, devastating events.

You might ask:

How could it be better? My loved one is gone.

I have been given six months to live.

I have been unemployed now for two years so how could it possibly be better?

These are undoubtedly difficult circumstances, but with Christ we can endure the difficult days because we have the knowledge that we are never alone. We can endure and succeed because we know God is protecting our heart and spirit. When my relationship with Christ is strong, I can still have joy, still have peace, still have contentment because I know my spirit is safe with the Lord no matter what my body may be going through. This is a huge source of comfort because we know that it is not our physical body that will reach eternity, but our spiritual body.

The only thing we have control over is how we will go through something, not always what we go through.

Having the master and creator of the universe protecting my eternity is the best way for me to maintain contentment and peace regardless of circumstances. I understand now that the statement, "I could not have made it without Jesus," means I could not have been able to maintain or return to my joy, peace, and contentment if I did not have a relationship with the Lord during my trouble. I am able to understand that my current situation does not determine my final destination. I must admit I sometimes get tired of always trying to hold on to my faith. It would be easier to allow the natural man to fill me with doubt, anger, and fear.

I did have doubts, *like: Will God allow me to live?*

I had anger: *I don't want to do this.*

And I had fear: *What am I about to experience with surgery and treatment?*

So, I reminded myself, *my current situation does not determine my final destination.* That lesson alone is profound and monumental. If going through trouble will help me focus more on the condition of my spirit, then the trouble was worth it. No matter the trial, no matter the challenge, no matter the loss, and no matter the cost, if we are able to forge a stronger relationship with the Lord through our trials, then the trouble was worth it. Even if you are diagnosed with cancer, developing the ability to focus on the condition of your spirit rather than your body makes the trouble worth it.

Recently, I watched a movie entitled *Take Care* in which a man said he suffered through cancer for two years and he hated it. He said he did not get any deep understanding, life lessons, or great wisdom from his experience. All he knew was he hated every minute of it, and consequently did not want to be around anyone who reminded him of that time in his life, including his mother and the ex-girlfriend who took care of him. Interestingly, the ex-girlfriend's friends nicknamed him "The Devil," because he broke up with her right after she nursed him back to health. What an appropriate name for this behavior, not because of what he did to the girlfriend but because of his lack of insight during his illness. In his attempt to distance himself from the pain of his illness he instead ran away from the love, affection, and support that carried him through it.

When my relationship with Christ is strong, I can still have joy, still have peace, still have contentment because I know my spirit is safe with the Lord no matter what my body may be going through.

It is Satan who hinders us from seeing God in the midst of our struggles. The devil is ecstatic when we miss opportunities to be more like Christ. When my personal character is dominated by negativity and characteristics like anger, bitterness, or hatred, there is a very high probability I have missed opportunities to see God. I have missed the opportunities that presented themselves to me to acknowledge God's presence in my life. Instead, in those moments I have succumbed to Satan's goal to tether my soul with his. Satan wins when we choose negativity over following the light of Christ. Satan wins when we keep our mind focused on what we don't want rather than accept God's will, which is to focus on how to get through the trials and be better for going through it.

Persistence and perseverance help us get through trials and help us to preserve our relationship with God. I have always liked the saying, "Don't cry over spilled milk." It is already done, and no amount of crying is going to put the milk back into the container. I get frustrated with parents who yell at children for dropping, breaking, or spilling something. No amount of yelling is going to repair whatever is broken or spilled, so why not take the opportunity to teach the importance of being careful without attacking the child's self-esteem? This perspective applies to many situations in life. For me, the cancer was here and there was nothing I could do to change that so there was no need crying, fretting, or worrying about the cancer or the outcome. I saw no point in dwelling on that fact, so I put it behind me, and I focused on the opportunity to press on and persevere.

As a Christian, my cancer outcome was in God's hands and not the doctor's. I could have had the best treatment available but if God had decided that this was my time to die, then there was nothing a man-made treatment could do to change the outcome God chose for me. There are many Christians with cancer who have gone through all the medical procedures and God determined it was time for their physical journey to end and their heavenly journey to begin.

No matter the trial, no matter the challenge, no matter the loss, and no matter the cost, if we are able to forge a stronger relationship with the Lord through our trials, then the trouble was worth it.

Have you ever heard the saying, "Your attitude affects your altitude?" The higher and closer to God my thoughts are, the better I can maintain a Christian attitude or perspective about my situation. In those moments when it seems bleak, and the doctors give you bad news, hold tightly to your belief that God is able, God's got you, and God has a plan for your life. It is through these practices God can protect us, He can walk with us. We have to be actively elevating our thoughts so God can protect our spirit. If we leave our spirit in the world, then the lion roaming around this world looking for whom he can devour will eventually start to inch closer and closer to us.

A minister recently said, "I can be sad and grieving over circumstances of this life and my spirit can be content and resting in the bosom of our Lord." What this means to me is that a physical trial or dilemma does not always equate to a spiritual trial. Just because you are going through something physically or situationally does not mean you are weak spiritually, or you will become weak. It simply means you are going through something, like every other person in the world. Every single human being will have trials, the Bible guarantees it. Why do you think the Bible talks so much about overcoming them? Why would we need so much guidance on how to deal with trials if we were not going to be pestered with them throughout our lives? Those physical trials are not a reflection of your spiritual wellbeing, but your spiritual wellbeing will determine how effectively and efficiently you go through those trials. Will you be defeated by the trials of this world or energized to praise God even more for protecting your spirit?

This is the attitude I hope others were able to see in me during my journey, and hopefully that is what resonated so much with them. This observation may be better stated as, "I see the power of God being displayed through you in the way you endure your trial." Yes, this is more accurate because in those moments of doubt and fear I tried to remember to go to God in prayer requesting His strength to carry me through.

In those times in the emergency room, I tried to keep my mind focused on praising God through prayer and silent singing. In one instance, Ernie and I were singing quietly together as we waited for surgery. Even though I thought we were singing quietly, both the nurse and the doctor commented that they enjoyed what we were singing. Even that was a gift from God to me to let me know that my doctor was a believer. It's always comforting to me to learn that a staff member who was attending to me physically was a believer. We were able to give God glory together in those moments of vulnerability.

Persistence and perseverance help us get through trials and help us to preserve our relationship with God.

This is another example of God blessing us by providing what we need when we need it, and who we need when we need it. God puts people in your life to minister to you. God removes people out of your life that are detrimental. God opens doors He wants you to go through and closes doors He does not want you to go through. Whatever your trouble is, God has allowed it because there are lessons He wants you to learn from your trouble. With a positive spiritual attitude, you can look for these lessons. But if you hate every moment of your trouble, you will miss the lessons.

This passage talks about the mindset to strive for when suffering trials.

I will praise the Lord at all times. I will constantly speak his praises. I will boast only in the Lord; let all who are helpless take heart. Come, let us tell of the Lord's greatness; let us exalt his name together. I prayed to the Lord, and he answered me. He freed me from all my fears. Those who look to him for help will be radiant with joy; no shadow of shame will darken their faces. In my desperation I prayed, and the Lord listened; he saved me from all my troubles. For the angel of the Lord is a guard: he surrounds and defends all who fear him. Psalms 34:1-7 (NLT).

The only way to understand this passage is with spiritual glasses. With carnal glasses this passage says God will save you from all of your troubles. But with spiritual glasses this passage says God will save you from all of your "spiritual troubles." If this referred to physical troubles, then no one would ever die and no one would ever get sick.

Dear friends, don't be surprised at the fiery trials you are going through, as if something strange were happening to you. Instead, be very glad—for these trials make you partners with Christ in His suffering, so you will have the wonderful joy of seeing his glory when it is revealed to all the world. I Peter 4:12-13 (NLT).

I love this passage because it tells me the attitude I should have when trouble comes. It says, "Don't be surprised... as if something strange were happening to you!" It is not strange to go through trouble, it is normal and expected! With this attitude, when trouble came, I was able to accept that it was just my turn.

This is not always easy when you are going through struggles and tribulations but trust me, you will be so much better spiritually if you are able to do so.

Those physical trials are not a reflection of your spiritual wellbeing, but your spiritual wellbeing will determine how effectively and efficiently you go through those trials.

Your attitude determines your altitude. If you are set on hating every minute of your trouble and asking, "Why me?" then you will be worse off mentally and spiritually when your trouble is over. If you seek God's face every step of the way, then you will see God and be thankful for His presence during and after your trouble is over.

Your Lessons Learned

1. What can I gain from this situation that will help me develop characteristics that will make me a better human being?

____

____

____

____

2. What can I learn and pass on to the next person that may walk this way?

____

____

____

____

3. How can I meditate on Christ and what He may have felt while going through His troubles for me?

____

____

____

____

Eight

The Restoration

And the God of all grace, who called you to His eternal glory in Christ, after you have suffered a little while, will Himself restore you and make you strong, firm, and steadfast. To Him be the power for ever and ever. Amen. 1 Peter 5:10 (NLT).

I can hardly describe the emotions I felt when I completed my last chemotherapy treatment. I was overwhelmed with joy, enveloped in relief, filled with praise, and even that does not do the feeling justice. My daughter decorated my chemotherapy room and the house for when I returned. I entered the clinic with a party hat on and passed out cookies to the staff. The clinic I attended did not have a bell on the wall like many other clinics. That did not stop me because I brought my own bell. When I left my last treatment, I rang my bell every step of the way and announced to every person I saw, "I finished chemotherapy!" with a smile and tears of joy on my face. Even the parking staff clapped for me! My mother and sister came to the house, and I fell into their arms with tears flowing because I was done, and they had been part of my village for every treatment and issue that arose. To say I was happy is just an echo of the rush of adrenaline I had.

I was already planning when I would return to all of my activities including exercising, gardening, hiking, running errands, woodworking, and anything else my heart desired to do. I ignorantly thought that in a few weeks I would be restored to my original health and physical abilities. After two weeks I came to realize my restoration would take much longer than I anticipated. What I had not planned for, were the side effects of treatment that lingered long after I rang my bell down the hallway passing out cookies. It took months for my blood to totally recover and provide the strength I needed to do all of my pre-cancer activities. That was difficult for me. I absolutely hated the fact I did not spring back into the action I so dearly missed. I thought I was finally finished with this, just for it to linger on and on. I began to think about restoration Biblically. In I Peter 5:10 it says,

"After you have suffered a little while, God will himself restore you and make you strong, firm, and steadfast," I Peter 5:10 (NLT).

What I find interesting is God does not wait for you to ask for or indicate you need restoration. God knows that after every event of suffering as a Christian we need restoration. This is a reminder of how loving God is toward us. He provides what we need before we know we need it. It is confirmation God is always watching. It does not matter if your challenge is a spiritual battle or a physical one. As a Christian, every battle requires the same Godly characteristics to overcome and win. In every battle, physical or spiritual, we need to go to God in prayer. We need to continue praising and depending on Him.

Honestly, I was tired and angry I was still having to deal with this. This battle wore me out and my praise got quieter. I had no desire to be around people because I was losing my positive demeanor. But God does not allow us to be tempted with more than we can bear, and after we have carried the burden, He provides restoration for our souls. Even James says,

Submit yourselves therefore to God. Resist the devil, and he will flee from you. James 4:7 (NLT).

This is a promise from God. This is God providing restoration after Satan attacks. Restoration begins when Satan flees. I am thankful God knows more about me than I know about myself because I felt I was at my limit after treatment number three, but God knew better.

Self-evaluation is very important in our Christian journey. Without it we may think we are doing just fine, but in reality, we are far from God's plan for our lives.

I heard a story once about two lumberjacks. A young lumberjack wanted to compete with an old timer lumberjack to see who could cut down the most trees in a certain amount of time. Both lumberjacks started at the same time, but the old timer would stop every hour to rest. To this the youngster laughed thinking to himself this was going to be an easy race for him to win. By the end of the specified time, the old timer cut down more trees than the youngster. The youngster was perplexed and angry and asked how that was even possible when he continued chopping and never took a break. The old timer explained that every time he stopped to rest, he also sharpened the blade of his ax. So, although the youngster was working very hard, he was working with dull tools, and he was expending much more energy than was necessary with a dull ax. The old timer took the time to restore his strength and restore his ax to its optimal condition allowing him to be more efficient in his work and cut down more trees in the same amount of time.

Jesus speaks about the need for restoration in Matthew 14. After Jesus fed 5,000 people and the disciples dispensed the food and cleaned up afterward, Jesus sent them away while he dispersed the crowd.

Immediately after this, Jesus insisted that his disciples get back into the boat and cross to the other side of the lake, while he sent the people home. Matthew 14:22 (NLT).

In another instance after the disciples worked very hard, Jesus took them away to get rest.

Then, because so many people were coming and going that they did not even have a chance to eat, he said to them, "Come with me by yourselves to a quiet place and get some rest." So they went away by themselves in a boat to a solitary place. Mark 6:31-32 (NLT).

God knows that after every event of suffering as a Christian we need restoration. This is a reminder of how loving God is toward us. He provides what we need before we know we need it.

After reading this I wondered, *who needs restoration after an attack, or after you have been on the battlefield using your weapons to defend against all enemies and all situations.* I thought about my situation, and I was very intent on responding Christlike to every comment of concern. What I mean is I tried not to dwell on my symptoms but on the power of God to heal my symptoms. At every emergency room visit I focused on God's goodness and prayed a prayer of thanksgiving believing He would provide what I needed. The other option is to worry about the outcome and be angry with God that you are in this situation. While in treatment I often thought of those who were praying for me and that gave me some comfort. Keeping your mind focused on the right things can be draining. Sometimes it seems like it is much easier to be negative and worrisome about your trials.

When James said resist the devil and he will flee, resistance takes effort, and it can be draining if you find yourself resisting for long periods of time. So even though we may feel fine, God has determined that after we suffer for a while we need restoration, and he will provide it for us. In I Peter 5:10, it says,

"God will restore your strength, and your ability to stand firm and steadfast," (NLT).

Restoration is a reprieve from the battlefield, a reprieve from the attacks. This does not mean you will not be attacked again, but God will provide time for you to be restored and get ready for the next attack. If God said He will restore our strength, it is because trials weaken us even if we do not acknowledge that we have been weakened. Our pride often interferes with our ability to recognize that we need restoration. Our pride says, "I am fine," but God says you need to be restored, and who would know better than Him? I also believe restoration is a time for us to evaluate our performance during the last attack by asking questions like:

Did I respond in a Christlike manner or is this an area that needs to be refined?

Did I keep my mind on Godly thoughts?

Finally, brothers, whatever is true, whatever is noble, whatever is right, whatever is pure, whatever is lovely, whatever is admirable - if anything is excellent or praiseworthy think about such things. Philippians 4:8 (NLT).

This is a very powerful verse for me. This is God's remedy for mind control. Hypnotists practice a form of mind control in that once hypnotized a person is at the mercy of the hypnotist to determine their behavior. With God's mind control, it is up to us to take control of our thoughts so that we are not at the mercy of Satan who wants to control our behavior. It is necessary to think about things objectively, and it is our choice how we choose to think, feel, and process those facts. Our thoughts and feelings are what affect our demeanor.

If you are a complainer that has something negative to say about every situation, consider meditating on Philippians 4:8 and replace your complaints with thoughts about truth, purity, loveliness, etcetera. I have been a complainer in the past but now I realize every single thing that happens, good or bad, is part of God's plan somehow. I have learned to consider God might be doing something in this situation and my complaining is interfering with God's plan. Imagine if instead of complaining you just stood still, with your mouth closed, and watched God work. It is amazing to just watch God work and come to the understanding that all your complaining does not change God's plan, it only changes your attitude about the plan.

Restoration is a reprieve from the battlefield, a reprieve from the attacks. This does not mean you will not be attacked again, but God will provide time for you to be restored and get ready for the next attack.

I have said before that we cannot always determine what we go through, but how we go through, and that applies to how we go through restoration as well. When you were going through restoration:

Were you able to draw on scripture for your strength?

Will you need to study more in order to have more scripture at your disposal?

Did pride interfere with your ability to receive help from others?

Self-evaluation is very important in our Christian journey. Without it we may think we are doing just fine, but in reality, we are far from God's plan for our lives. I had to ask, *what happens if God chooses not to heal me? Does this mean God does not love me, or I am somehow in sin?* No, it does not mean this at all. But there are times God chooses for us to stay in our situation, and we may be in our situation until we die. How does one deal with that?

I will boast only in the LORD; let all who are helpless take heart. Come, let us tell of the LORD's greatness; let us exalt his name together. I prayed to the LORD, and he answered me. He freed me from all my fears. Psalms 34:2-4 (NLT).

Some troubles are chronic, and they may never go away. I do not refer to any type of violence, abuse, or criminal activity, but some physical conditions are chronic. For some poverty is chronic, the consequences of a poor education. When we can accept God has chosen for us to stay in our particular situation, then we ought to also pray God frees us from the fear that often accompanies our troubles. God will not always free you from your pain and suffering, but God will free you from your fears when you can keep your eyes focused on Him knowing that whatever you are going through, God's got you. This is a major shift in our thinking. We are believers but we are also mere humans.

Our spirit says, *"Pray."*

Our carnal side says, *"For how long?"*

Our spirit says, *"God's got this."*

Our carnal side says, *"But what if He doesn't?"*

Our carnal side says, *"Heal me. Fix my problem."*

Our spirit says, *"God knows what is best for you."*

This is so difficult! We all want healing and our problems to disappear. But honestly that may not be what is best for our spiritual walk.

I am reminded of the man at the Pool of Bethesda. After Jesus healed him, he told the man to go and sin no more. Was it sin that brought him to the pool looking for healing? Sin may have brought him to the pool but while he was waiting by the pool for healing, he probably was not sinning. We can receive eternal salvation with terminal diseases, with poverty, with trauma in our lives, and chronic pain, but we cannot receive salvation in sin. The carnal mind wants a perfectly happy life, but the spirit wants a relationship with God. I wanted to be restored from my cancer journey in two weeks, but God knew better. Whether I liked that decision from Him is irrelevant to the fact that his decisions are the superior alternative to all of my own wants and desires.

The carnal mind wants a perfectly happy life, but the spirit wants a relationship with God.

How does one receive restoration if the trouble never goes away, and in some situations will get worse leading to death, divorce, or unemployment? Restoration is available to you whenever you reach out for God's hand.

So let us come boldly to the throne of our gracious God. There we will receive his mercy, and we will find grace to help us when we need it most. Hebrews 4:16 (NLT).

Your physical trouble may never leave but your spirit has access to mercy and grace to help you through your troubling times.

That is why we never give up. Though our bodies are dying, our spirits are being renewed every day. For our present troubles are small and won't last very long. Yet they produce for us a glory that vastly outweighs them and will last forever! So we don't look at the troubles we can see now; rather, we fix our gaze on things that cannot be seen. For the things we see now will soon be gone, but the things we cannot see will last forever. 2 Corinthians 4:16-18 (NLT).

Your Lessons Learned

1. Review previous troubles and ask what can I do differently when the trouble comes again?

____
____
____
____

2. What can I do to keep good thoughts, Godly thoughts, in my mind?

____
____
____
____

3. Does my pride interfere with my ability to ask for and/or accept help? How can I strengthen my walk with the Lord so pride or other carnal characteristics will not interfere?

____
____
____
____

Nine

The Decision

Commit to the Lord whatever you do, and he will establish your plans. Proverbs 16:3 (NLT).

I was talking with my husband after I completed all my treatments, and he made the comment I had experienced the worst possible medical condition. I agreed with him, but I told him I was one of the fortunate ones because my experience would one day be in the past and a distant memory. I realized there is a whole population of people who experience chronic conditions. They are unable to experience the blessing of saying, "It is over." With every day that passed I became stronger, and my hair began to grow back. One day no one will know I had cancer unless I tell them.

I don't carry any visible marks of my time with cancer, but I know there are journeys and trials that leave scars on and in people forever. Even though I have not experienced it, I imagine losing a child creates a deep scar that changes the trajectory of your life forever. Chronic pain affects how you live your life every single day and can wear on not only your body but your mind and spirit. Divorce is final but the pain is deep, raw, and lasting.

How does someone find joy and peace when they must deal with that type of pain, and those circumstances forever?

How can you experience contentment when you never get a break from pain and suffering?

The challenge of it all stuck with me, so I decided to ask others how they cope with perpetual pain and challenges.

Mrs. Bronson is a dear friend who has suffered many losses in her life. She had to attend each of her siblings' funerals, all of whom were younger than her. She also was forced to bury both of her parents, her grandparents, her spouse, and her child. Despite all of the death she has seen, she continues on with an easy smile and an infectious laugh. She is not always cheerful, she admits to me, and also struggles with the loneliness that comes with loss. I asked what helped her during her darkest days. "I worked hard on myself," was her response. During that time, she focused on herself and activities to keep her mind occupied with something other than her losses. She maintained a schedule and looked forward to getting up and getting out of the house to stay active and engaged with the life around her.

If you are not in the habit of calling on the Lord during good and bad times, you will find it almost impossible to call on Him when you have no one else to call.

She maintained her social life and circle of friends and made a commitment to go whenever someone said, "Let's go." True, there were times when she did not want to go, but making that commitment helped her to get out of self and enjoy the company of her friends. Mrs. Bronson taught me that pain doesn't have to consume you, no matter how terrible and tragic it might be.

Some people might not think of divorce as a chronic condition, but I have seen the devastating and lasting effects it can have on people. Melissa is a friend who felt that devastation firsthand when her husband asked for a divorce after thirty years of marriage. She was totally blindsided and had no clue he was unhappy in the relationship. It took her several years to be okay. She called often with the same sentiment, "I don't understand why he did this." She would ruminate about different theories she had as to why. The effects of the decision her husband made were not quickly overcome, and they were not isolated to just the two of them. Divorce never affects only the husband and wife. The entire family was permanently affected by his actions.

Her faith and relationship with God also suffered during that time. I sadly saw a believer drift further and further away from God as her personal challenges, and the fallout from them, worsened. It appeared her spiritual ordeals intensified because her faith and priorities were anchored to the image of a happily married couple, and not as much on Jesus Christ. Thankfully, God was patient with her as she worked through the many different emotions she felt and remembered her foundation in the Lord. Contrastingly, my friend Jennifer also went through the pain of divorce. During her journey and battle one of the things I noticed as a key difference was that Jennifer held fast to her faith during that time. She made sure to prioritize every church service and Bible study, clinging to God as her marriage came to an end. I was impressed with her tenacity to hold on to her faith and be an example to her children and grandchildren. Jennifer and Melissa taught me that through every challenge no matter what it is, or how difficult it might be, to do my absolute best to cling to God during those waves.

Charise and Maya are two friends who also share hardships, but instead of divorce they both lost their adult sons to accidents. Charise will never get over the loss of her oldest son and her expressions of grief are just as deep today as they were fifteen years ago when he passed away. Her heart seems to be permanently broken and irreparable. I often wonder how she was able to parent her younger children after the tragedy. But, most likely, like other troubles we learn how to compartmentalize our pain and suffering so that we can function in life.

Maya, on the other hand, never talked about her loss unless she was asked directly about it. When I asked how she handled her loss she responded, "It was God." She talked about how all the members of the family handled their grief differently, and everyone was allowed to express their grief however they wanted. She has pictures of her son displayed in her house and finds herself talking to him at times. Yet, she was able to move on with life and enjoy life again despite her great and devastating loss. She continued her travels and had a strong group of friends who were a support for her.

It is interesting that in both of these tragedies the one who held tightly to their faith seemed to fare better than the other. Those who practice walking with God regularly have an easier time running to God during trouble. If you are not in the habit of calling on the Lord during good and bad times, you will find it almost impossible to call on Him when you have no one else to call.

Darlene and Charity, two sisters, who both suffer with chronic illnesses, are excellent examples of faith and dedication. In fact, the entire family of three sisters and their mother all have chronic pain and physical challenges. They are a wonder to me because of their commitment and perseverance to worshipping the Lord with all the strength that they can muster. I discovered when I interviewed them that much of their approach to their suffering is learned behavior from their parents who also suffered with chronic pain from the time the women were very young. They saw their father keep moving despite his heart condition and other illnesses. They heard wisdom from a very young age like:

"The Lord will provide."

"Don't let anyone steal your joy."

"God always provides a ram in the thicket."

I asked, "What about when you are in real pain and can't even get out of the bed, what do you think then?"

Charity responded, "While in pain I often pray, Lord help me through this pain because I don't know what you want from me."

She also said, it is perfectly fine to say on any given day, "I can only do what I can do. If I can push through the pain I will, but if not, I accept today will be a 'Be still and know I am God' day."

She added, "Even in pain there is always something to be thankful for."

Darlene added she sings gospel songs often and tries to laugh and joke as much as possible. She stated, "You have to make your own self happy." This statement is simple but powerful and I believe it can help in any and all suffering situations. We cannot depend on someone else to make us happy because when that person is gone, your source of happiness vanishes. When a husband leaves from divorce or death, if the wife's happiness was dependent on the husband, then she will have a hard time regaining her joy. If your happiness is based on your physical abilities, then when your health fails, you will have nothing to base your happiness on.

You may say, "Keep the spiritual gift and give me my health back." Or you can accept that this is your journey and look for opportunities to praise God through your pain.

I used to visit an elderly woman named Mrs. Mason. One day I was complaining about being tired and overwhelmed by raising my four children who were young at the time. Mrs. Mason was a paraplegic and spent most of her time in her bed which faced a window.

She looked at her window and said, "I thank God for that window because through it I can see and feel the warmth from the sun. I thank God for the sun, and I thank God every day for waking up in my right mind."

Her comment struck my heart and I never complained about my life again. Whenever I think I want to complain, I think about Mrs. Mason who was just thankful to be alive. I have so much in my life to be thankful for. Worrying seems like a slap in God's face.

God is so patient with us, though. He allows us to express our frustrations then sends someone like Mrs. Mason to teach us a simple but powerful lesson. I recently read Job again and with my new perspective on life post chemotherapy, I am exceptionally thankful that Job is in the Bible. Job's life is an excellent example of suffering, grief, depression, physical pain, acceptance, and trusting in God. Job was in excruciating pain:

I would rather be strangled— rather die than suffer like this. I hate my life and don't want to go on living. Oh, leave me alone for my few remaining days. Job 7:15 (NLT).

Have your troubles ever made you feel like Job? Has the pain ever been so great and overwhelming you considered, even if just for a moment, I would rather die than continue to endure what I am dealing with? Pain, whether physical or mental, can be so great that all you can think of is how to make it stop. Job got to that point where he believed he could not endure anymore suffering. Job was tired of trying to present himself a certain way when all he felt was pain and abandonment by his friends.

If I decided to forget my complaints, to put away my sad face and be cheerful, I would still dread all the pain, for I know you will not find me innocent, O God. Whatever happens, I will be found guilty. So what's the use of trying? Job 9:27-29 (NLT).

Job is in the depths of despair and is ready to give up. He sees no way out of this situation and is ready to forfeit everything. He is tired of wearing a smile on his face to please others, and he believes nothing will turn God's hand toward blessing him again.

Job spends some time trying to understand what he had done to deserve this punishment.

"I am disgusted with my life. Let me complain freely. My bitter soul must complain. I will say to God, 'Don't simply condemn me– tell me the charge you are bringing against me. What do you gain by oppressing me? Why do you reject me, the work of your own hands, while smiling on the schemes of the wicked?" Job 10:1-3 (NLT).

This is very similar to questions we ask ourselves in times of trouble, like *what have I done to deserve this?* Sometimes our troubles are consequences of our behaviors. Many health conditions are directly related to how we care for our bodies. Poor budgeting and money management will cause financial hardships. Arrogance and bitterness may lead to loneliness.

On the other hand, just like Job, sometimes our troubles have nothing to do with our behaviors. Job asks,

"Why doesn't the Almighty bring the wicked to judgment? Why must the Godly wait for him in vain?" Job 24:1 (NLT).

This indicates to me that Job is confused about why he is suffering when he has not done anything to deserve punishment. I have had this same thought about why the unsaved seem to have it all and many Godly people seem to struggle. I especially like I Peter 4:12 as a response to that question.

Dear friends, don't be surprised at the fiery trials you are going through, as if something strange were happening to you. Instead, be very glad—for these trials make you partners with Christ in His suffering, so you will have the wonderful joy of seeing His glory when it is revealed to all the world.

When you cannot find a reason for your pain and suffering, this verse can give you comfort. It can help you put your trouble in the right context and look for opportunities to glorify God through your suffering. Especially if your suffering is a permanent condition in this physical body. It reminds us that our experiences can give us the opportunity to partner with Christ in His suffering, to experience a small fraction of what He suffered for us. I wonder if Jesus suffered from chronic physical pain that was not recorded. Would his behaviors, words, and example change? With this thought in mind, I have greater confidence in the ability to be like Christ even during the storms of life.

Those who have chronic conditions have the unique opportunity to develop a level of spirituality that is not available to those who do not have chronic conditions. My cancer journey gave me unique opportunities that others may never experience. I encourage you to acknowledge this special spiritual gift God has blessed you with that allows you to endure the suffering and glorify God in spite of your suffering. You are an example to others. You may say, "Keep the spiritual gift and give me my health back." Or you can accept that this is your journey and look for opportunities to praise God through your pain.

At least I can take comfort in this: Despite the pain, I have not denied the words of the Holy One. Job 6:10 (NLT).

Your Lessons Learned

1. What decision can you make that will lead to more joy in your life?

2. If you have allowed a traumatic event or chronic condition to decide your current outlook on life, how would you like your outlook to be different?

3. What decision can be made about improving your relationship with the Lord?

Ten

The Choice

And now, dear brothers and sisters, one final thing. Fix your thoughts on what is true, and honorable, and right, and pure, and lovely, and admirable. Think about things that are excellent and worthy of praise. Philippians 4:8 NLT

The word cancer appeared again in my life, but this time it was not for me but for my loved ones. My sister-friend, Heather, who became my cancer buddy as we fought our cancer together was diagnosed with a recurrence eight months after her last chemotherapy treatment. I was devastated. Her treatment would be even more aggressive and harsher on her body than the first time. I immediately felt a sense of confusion in my soul and the questions formed.

Why Lord?

Why her and not me?

How do I express gratitude I am cancer free, and my dear friend must go through this again?

Will my presence in her life right now bring her joy or resentment toward me?

Another friend, Patsy, had my same diagnosis at the same time, but only required surgery and no chemotherapy. However, six months later the cancer returned and now the treatment included chemotherapy and radiation. When we spoke her first question was, "Why me?"

I had a similar question, "Why her and not me?" I became angry because it all seemed so random to me. Nothing about a recurrence for one and not the other makes sense. There is nothing about me that is different from these other ladies. All of us have devoted our lives to living for Christ to the best of our abilities.

If this is all random, why pray at all?

Why worship at all?

Why make any effort to please God when He won't even protect us from more suffering?

There are several scriptures that tell us to pray for protection. Then why Lord are you not protecting us, especially those who have already suffered, whether from loss or illness or some other trouble?

As I pondered these things, I realized I was experiencing the anger that many experience with their own suffering. I did not feel this level of anger with my diagnosis, but it was very real as I faced cancer again through my friends.

And then the unthinkable happened. A third friend, Olivia, was diagnosed with a recurrence in July and died eight weeks later. She had been cancer free for three years. When I was diagnosed, she shared her experiences with me, and I appreciated her for it. Olivia was younger than me and did not have the opportunity to see her grandchildren grow up, or other milestones that we all hold dear. She too was sincere in her walk with the Lord. Again, I felt angry at the random nature of all of this. None of this made sense. In my version of fairness, it is not fair that anyone who suffers from a trial should ever have to go through it again. But if I open this can of fairness then I cannot stop with cancer. Nothing in this life is fair. I resigned myself to this very sad fact, fairness has nothing to do with life. Yet my human mind still shouts, it is not fair that someone who strives to live for Christ must suffer the same as someone who is not trying to live a Godly life. If we who are trying so hard to live Godly receive no extra divine protection from human suffering, then why try at all?

The reality slapped me hard in the face: there is divine protection from human suffering, but the protection is promised for the spirit not for the body. The body will suffer and that is a real and ugly realization that we cannot run from. The only choice we have is to run to God to protect our spirit or run away from God and endure spiritual suffering in addition to the physical. How quickly one chooses to run to God is directly related to one's intimacy with Him.

Like any relationship, you call on those you feel a closeness to. Those you speak to regularly will know the trouble in your life before those you see on occasion. The same principle applies to our relationship with the Lord. The more you interact with God through His word, prayer, and praise, the more quickly you will run to Him for comfort. I also understand that one only recognizes the need to make this choice when you are faced with trouble, otherwise, you would have no reason to think about this. This strengthens my belief that trouble is necessary. Thank God for trouble! It is only through trouble you come to this crossroad where this choice must be made.

The only choice we have is to run to God to protect our spirit or run away from God and endure spiritual suffering in addition to the physical.

As I grieved the difficult journey ahead for my two friends and the too early death of Olivia, I had to look hard for God.

Where are you God?

What is your plan?

What is the purpose of all of this?

How are we to find you when everything seems senseless?

How are we to give you glory in the midst of all of this pain?

This taught me another hard lesson, God will not be found in the molecules and cells of the flesh. Yes, He made the flesh but that is not where He resides. God is where the spirit and soul reside.

I thank God for the physical blessings He has allowed me to enjoy, but I must be fully committed to the belief that without physical blessings God is still worthy of all praise because I believe I will receive the gift of eternal life when this physical body fails, or when life does not look like the perfect lives portrayed in fiction. So, I think of Olivia, and I can have a warm feeling because I believe she is at peace with the Lord. She may have missed out on the physical blessing of growing old, but she has received the bigger blessing of being in the presence of God. So, I am sad for her and her family. But I am also happy for her because she made it to paradise where I hope to see her again one day.

But what about Heather and Patsy? How do I glorify God through what they must face again?

I have to consider they will survive or they will not.

How do I consider their possible death and not feel a sense of guilt I am alive with no recurrence thus far?

It takes all of my focus to keep my mind on Jesus and not on the fear that tries to creep into my mind.

But why focus on Jesus when I have already concluded that this is all random?

I have decided to choose to focus on Jesus because the alternative is too dark and depressing.

Without the hope of eternal life, the random nature of this life is dreadful. I cannot count on anything that this life has to offer because it can all be gone in an instant. But eternal life is mine and no physical trial on this earth can take that away from me. Now that is something to give God praise for. I choose to meditate on this fact and with this focus I can have a sense of calm for Heather and Patsy because I know they too have eternal life. I cannot give any plausible explanation for their current trials of recurrence, and I can only give the very unsatisfying answer, "Only God knows."

This is unsatisfactory to my human mind that shouts this is unfair. But to my spirit this simple answer brings peace. The older and wiser I get, the more satisfying this answer is. The older and wiser I get the more I understand I understand nothing! After all of my questions, frustrations, fits of anger and confusion I have concluded once again I do not have all the answers, but I serve a God who does.

There are some who are faced with similar questions and conclude there is no God. Yet when I very briefly considered this answer my heart began to feel very heavy with the weight of the world. It is too much for me to consider all the pain and suffering in this world is for nothing. There has to be an answer that allows me to have hope in something outside of myself, outside of this very ugly and cruel world. I suppose if I were wealthy, it would be easier to believe there is no God because money would buy any physical comforts I may want.

I heard a young man on television say he concluded there was no God because his father died suddenly, and he could not make sense of this. I believe many come to this conclusion when it seems their prayers go unanswered. Sometimes as believers we also struggle with this concept. We logically think if *I pray hard and long, and let the tears flow, God will see my sincerity and answer my prayer favorably.* But Jesus also prayed well into the night, and He prayed so hard His sweat appeared as droplets of blood. I have never prayed that hard, and still His conclusion was, "Not my will, but thine."

After all of my questions, frustrations, fits of anger and confusion I have concluded once again I do not have all the answers, but I serve a God who does.

If God answered, "No" to His only Son, the perfect lamb of God who never committed a sin, why did I think all of my prayers should be answered, "Yes?" When Jesus raised Lazarus from the dead, Lazarus just died again because it is appointed unto man to die. If everyone must die, then everyone must suffer disease or tragedy. The act of dying is tragic.

Like Jesus, we must choose God's will above our own. We only see the physical, but God sees the beginning and the end. God sees the hearts of man. God sees our past and what is in our future. God's ultimate goal for each of us is not physical comfort but spiritual salvation. Since I cannot see what God sees, I have to put all of my trust in Him and conclude, "Not my will, but thine."

Once my trust was securely in the Lord, I chose to smile often, laugh often, breathe in hope, and breathe out fear. I chose to intentionally be thankful for today with all the opportunities and trials today brings.

Your Lessons Learned

1. What are you or have you been angry with God for?

____

____

____

____

2. How has God disappointed you? What prayer did He not answer?

____

____

____

____

3. What choice can you make that will give you peace?

____

____

____

____

Epilogue

Thank you for allowing me to share my journey with you. It was cathartic for me, and I hope it was insightful for you. My hope and prayer for writing this book is most of all God would be glorified and you may consider the lessons God is trying to teach you through your journeys just as I found a few through mine. I am convinced that when we change our perspective toward our storms, we will weather them with much more peace, hope, and love. Instead of asking, "Why me?" consider asking, "What lessons can I learn through this storm?" Be intentional about looking for God's hand in your life. The more we look for God the more we will find Him.

Although this book is about what lessons God revealed to me, I am excited for you to find your own lessons God is waiting to teach you. My journey has made me more empathetic to others who are hurting no matter what their struggle is. I thought I was being still and waiting on God, but I learned I was still holding the rudder and trying to make this ship turn the way I wanted it to. I am much more in tune to the many ways God blesses us, and how some of those ways have gone severely unnoticed. Although you must own your own journey, please remember you are not fighting alone. The battle is not yours only, but it is all those in your life who love you, and most importantly you have the greatest warrior possible on your team fighting for you. Let people into your space. We pride ourselves on being able to handle everything and not needing anyone. But I have learned there are great blessings awaiting you when you let people in.

I have great empathy for those who do not have a village. In my online cancer support group, I felt overwhelming sadness for the women who lived alone with no family or good friends. They worked full-time because there was no one else to help financially. I encourage you to reach out to someone because God did not intend for us to go through our storms alone. Consider the church as a place to meet some really good people. My church family is an extension of my biological family. It is often said that the church family is closer than the biological family. This can be true and challenging if your biological family does not live by the same belief system you live by.

Like I said before, "Your attitude determines your altitude." This is especially true when enduring troubling times. What you choose to focus on determines whether your mind will be on the ground focused on all the dirty negative perceptions, or if your mind will be in the blue skies focused on warmth, love, and God's grace. Sometimes to get through very difficult dark days, all you have are the promises of God to hold you close as you go through whatever you are going through.

After you have gone through your storm take time to be restored. No one is infallible and everyone gets tired. Take time to breathe, to enjoy the wonders of God's creation, and to allow God to heal and rejuvenate your spirit. Sometimes people refuse to believe they need restoration and end up in the emergency room because their stress, anxiety, or depression is manifesting itself in bodily symptoms. Don't be so quick to return to your previous life activities. Actually, there is no previous life to return to because after you have weathered a storm your life will not ever look the same. It will look better.

Even if you have chronic problems or health conditions, you have the opportunity for your spirit to be better. And that is what we are all striving for, for our spirit to look more and more like Christ.

About the Author

My name is Marcia (Mar-see-a) and I love the Lord. I have been married for thirty-nine years and I have four adult children. I am a licensed marriage and family therapist, and a licensed clinical social worker. God has blessed me again to receive a job in an area I absolutely love. I now work as a field medical social worker providing service to many of our most vulnerable and underserved citizens. I began teaching the Bible when my children were in kindergarten because I wanted to ensure they were being stimulated spiritually. As they progressed in grade, I progressed right along with them. I thought it was great. My kids may have another viewpoint. I asked to lead a Ladies' Bible Class once, and since then I have had many opportunities to share with other women the lessons God reveals to me as he molds me. I have come to love sharing God's word with others through personal Bible studies and speaking at seminars. The most exciting part of teaching is to see the spark of understanding and application of God's word in the lives of others. Please visit my website and follow me on social media:

realtalkandrealwalk@gmail.com

Instagram: @realtalkandrealwalk

Facebook: realtalkandrealwalk

Twitter: realtalk_walk

Realtalkandrealwalk.com